Parts of the Foreword to Revised and Augmented (Seventh) Edition

RECENTLY I listened with interest and some pleasure to a B.B.C. feature on hypnotism, and to the incorporated comments by Dr. Alexander Kennedy, Professor of Psychological Medicine at Durham University. Previously the B.B.C. had sponsored fantastic and injurious representations anent hypnotism. The comments of Dr. Kennedy were different. Professedly they were not only rational but thoroughly up-to-date. Nevertheless, substantially they were but little more than echoes of statements by me in an article entitled "Hypnotism: What it Is and What it Does", published in the *Weekly Times and Echo* as long ago as 28th October, 1911. The conclusions I put forward were results of the nine-years' investigation and experimentation terminated by me in 1909, *the very year in which Dr. Alexander Kennedy was born*. *Rational Hypnotism*, wherein I gave my views in detail, was completed in 1910 but was not published until April, 1914. The manuscript had passed through the hands of many publishers who rejected it because its then-unorthodox contents conflicted strongly with the views of accredited "authorities." I therefore felt impelled to convince some of those "authorities" of the truth of my contentions; and, fortunately, I succeeded. Among these was the world-famous alienist and neurologist, Dr. L. Forbes Winslow, of whose frank and courageous attitude under the circumstances I could not speak too highly. The eventual publication of *Rational*

Hypnotism served many useful ends, and 1929 saw the first edition of the present work—a work particularly intended for the general public. This edition differs slightly from its predecessors, but never as regards theoretical principles.

Whoever calmly and judiciously considers the contents of this book will scarcely be inclined to believe that hypnotism *allows* of the domination claimed for it by practitioners blinded by their own egotism. Hypnotism is mainly a matter of co-operation, and the duty of myself or any other hypnotic operator does not —indeed cannot—consist in attempting to override desires of, nor foist convictions on, clients or others. Hypnotism is not foolproof (what is?), but when used judiciously it powerfully favours freedom inasmuch as, by revealing and cultivating latent capacities, it increases efficiency of thought and action, and also fosters the courage requisite for dogged adherence to what one considers right.

"Things are only worth what one makes them worth," wrote Moliére. I am gratified to find that, as ardently hoped, rational hypnotism is being sought for ensuring and facilitating readjustments in marital, domestic, and social relations, and for fostering the equipment that spells for so many success and progress in the professional and business domains. I am further gratified that this book awakened many persons to a recognition of the means whereby certain of their handicaps and shortcomings were successfully combated.

Over a century ago daily papers occasionally announced confinements as having occurred "pain-

HYPNOTISM MADE PRACTICAL

By

J. LOUIS ORTON

" The mind of man is far from the nature of a clear and equal glass, wherein the beams of things should reflect according to their true incidence; nay, it is rather like an enchanted glass, full of superstition and imposture, if it be not delivered and reduced."

" A cripple in the right way will out-distance a racer in the wrong way."

—FRANCIS, LORD BACON.

Foreword by

MELVIN POWERS

1969 EDITION

Wilshire Book Company
12015 Sherman Road
No. Hollywood, California 91605

Revised and Augmented (Eighth) Edition
Ninth Edition, January 1951
Reprinted January 1952
Tenth Edition, January 1955

Originally published in Great Britain
First published in U.S.A.
December 1957

Printed in the United States of America

FOREWORD

Any hypnotist who can arrange a post-hypnotic delivery for an expectant mother, so that later she reports, "During the actual birth the sensations I had were of sheer delight," merits serious attention.

Author J. Louis Orton, on page 98, lists fifty different ways in which hypnotism can be beneficially employed. He tells of many such cases that he, himself, successfully treated by using hypnosis. We have here no mere theorist, but a practical man of action. He states that hypnotism belongs to the subject of psychology, and that hypnotism's early history (linking it with hysteria, mob psychology and spiritism) was most unfortunate.

This English author shows us why the subconscious must exist; how this "mental selective and inventive power" is always at work in sorting out and arranging the ideas which achieve consciousness. For example, when asked if you know Mogie Berenson, and you don't, your mind must scan its entire content of acquaintances before you say, "No." This kind of supplementary work is always going on so that consciousness may exist.

A clear and simple account of why unpleasant emotions are bad for you is found in chapter 8, "Why Thought Kills or Cures." Emotions, by means of the ductless glands, can generate poisonous compounds which reach the entire system through the blood. Anger can change the properties of saliva, etc. Simple experiments have proved the dangers lurking in unpleasant emotions. For example, 80 out of 100 persons were violently ill after hearing they had been given an emetic (a medicine inducing vomiting) by mistake. Actually, the emetic was only sugared water, thus proving the power of emotion and mind over our health and well-being.

What makes HYPNOTISM MADE PRACTICAL especially worth reading are the new ideas in it, insights normally not found in similar books. Notably, the author shows the relation between hypnotism and genius. Hypnosis is "an artificially induced contemplative mood." The genius merely induces such moods naturally. Thus, the genius can achieve his remarkable effects because he is able to concentrate his attention to the fullest extent.

Astonishingly, J. Louis Orton says that hypnotism has a great future in moral reform. It can be used to regenerate the individual's "psychology." For instance, in the case of a juvenile delinquent, we can, through post-hypnotic suggestions, change the delinquent's warped line of thought.

Hypnosis can also be applied to the service of education, and has a definite place in the curriculum of the future. Its use in the fields of aviation, radio, television, and pedestrian safety is not only advocated, but expounded. The author has even experimented on television with mass-hypnosis. He advocates mass-suggestion broadcasts incorporating therapeutic suggestions.

HYPNOTISM MADE PRACTICAL also includes an excellent presentation of techniques for hypnotizing.

The impressive impact of this book is that it takes hypnotism off the vaudeville stage, out of the parlor, and into the clinic, the prison, the school room, and the home. It brings hypnotism, as one of the great medicines of the future, into the normal mind — where it has every right to be.

Melvin Powers

12015 Sherman Road
No. Hollywood, California 91605

lessly during mesmeric trance." About half a century later, Dr. (Mme.) Dobrovolsky, of Switzerland, reported one case in which, owing to post-hypnotic analgesia, suggested nine days earlier, confinement was practically painless. As long ago as 1911 my first case of the kind occurred, and the medical man who attended remarked: " I could not have got a more passive condition had I used chloroform." Since then I have had similar cases; and, as stated in my eleventh chapter, on one occasion I also acted as accoucheur. (Further details are given in my book on *Personality*.) However, a test case, under stringent conditions—including my absence from the mother—was recently conducted in connection with the *Daily Herald*. The applicant was " Jill Morrison " (Mrs. Anne S. Fraser, wife of Wing-Commander E. G. Fraser, M.V.O., A.F.C.), the paper's Beauty Expert, and the confinement took place at a maternity home. " Jill " had a strained heart, and therefore chloroform or other chemical anæsthetic was not favoured. Her medical man, though successful in other instances, was unable to induce hypnosis in her. (She informed me that she personally had done a little hypnotism, and been interested in the subject about six years.) At her first visit to me I induced hypnosis and gave appropriate suggestions regarding her pregnancy and confinement. At her second visit I suggested that whenever labour commenced she would recognize the various signs and without panic would journey to the maternity home. Two months passed, and within little more than one month the babe was due to arrive. Her published account stated:

" Feeling fine. Realize now that the suggestions have helped me right through my pregnancy. Am more vigorous than I ever was. Didn't even mind moving house recently. Can manage the steep hill which leads to my home without getting out of breath. Used to be highly strung. Now I'm very placid. Believe it or not, can still touch my toes without bending my knees."

Sixteen days after " Jill's " sixth and last treatment, Wing-Commander Fraser telephoned me; his wife, he said, had gone to the maternity home, labour having commenced, and that she was free from pain and was in high spirits. Miss Janet Grey, who is the *Daily Herald's* editress of matters relating to women's interests, was present during the whole of the confinement. Her published account stated: " I can vouch that she was obviously without any pain at all "; and " Jill Morrison's " ran: " Not being in pain, I was able to take a great interest in everything and enjoy the procedure. Because I wasn't complaining about being in pain when I arrived at the maternity home I had some difficulty in persuading them that I was so far on in labour. . . During the actual birth the sensations I had were of sheer delight. . . I saw him " (the babe) " immediately he was born and heard his first cry—factors which I understand are of major importance from a psychological point of view." *I* was not the informer and cannot vouch for the correctness of that notion!

27th November 1948 J. LOUIS ORTON

Preface to Tenth Edition

Five Months of the year 1949 were taken up by my invited professional tour of India. There I had the pleasure of meeting many important members of the Government—including that courageous and able statesman, Pundit Jawarharlal Nehru—and of lunching with our High Commissioner, Sir Archibald Nye, Lady Nye and their elder daughter, all of whom I found most interested in my work. Had time permitted, I would have availed myself of the invitations to lecture and demonstrate at the Universities of Calcutta, Madras and Hyderabad (where it had been arranged I should be given a civic welcome and be a state guest), as well as to the Medical and Dental Associations in those cities. At Bombay I addressed the officers of the All-India Radio station, whence my first broadcast occurred. My second and third broadcasts were from New Dehli, one before going to Simla, and one after my return from there. At Bombay my lecture-demonstration at the Grant Medical College was greeted with enthusiastic understanding by professors and students, as happened also at the Lady Hardinge Medical College and the Lady Irwin College. I also addressed the Tata Institution. At New Delhi I had the pleasure of lecturing and demonstrating—under the chairmanship of General Master—to the officers of the Army, the Navy and the Air Force and also to a few hundreds of medical men. On 27th April 1951 was published the first of three books which I was asked to write for India in the first place. It is entitled: " Auto-Suggestion: How to Master It " and deals comprehensively with auto-hypnotism. The publishers are D. B. Taraporevala Sons & Co. Ltd., of Bombay.

J. LOUIS ORTON,
10*th August* 1954.

" Kingsthorpe ",
Hawthorn Drive,
Willowbank, Uxbridge (Middx.).

CONTENTS

PAGE

FOREWORD 3, 4

CHAPTER I
THE RATIONAL ATTITUDE 11

CHAPTER II
SOME PERTINENT HISTORICAL FACTS 16

CHAPTER III
WHAT HYPNOTISM IS NOT 21

CHAPTER IV
THE "PHYSICAL" AND THE "MENTAL" 29

CHAPTER V
WHAT HYPNOTISM IS 36

CHAPTER VI
SUGGESTION AND AUTO-SUGGESTION 46

CHAPTER VII
CAN HYPNOTISM BE A CRIMINAL AGENT? 50

CHAPTER VIII
WHY THOUGHT KILLS AND CURES 57

CHAPTER IX
PREPARATORY EXPERIMENTS 67

CHAPTER X
THE INDUCTION AND TERMINATION OF HYPNOSIS 74

CHAPTER XI
THE MANAGEMENT OF HYPNOSIS 83

CHAPTER XII
MEDICAL AND SURGICAL USES 92

CHAPTER XIII
CO-OPERATIVE TREATMENT 99

CHAPTER XIV
MENTAL AND NERVOUS COMPLAINTS 108

CHAPTER XV
MORAL REFORM 119

CHAPTER XVI
EDUCATIONAL AND SOCIAL USES 128

CHAPTER XVII
MUSIC AND VOICE 136

CHAPTER XVIII
THE PLATFORM, THE PULPIT AND THE STAGE .. 146

CHAPTER XIX
SPEECH DEFECTS 150

CHAPTER XX
HYPNOTISM FROM NEW VIEWPOINTS (AVIATION, RADIO, TELEVISION, ETC.) 155

CHAPTER XXI
HYPNOTISM AND ROAD SAFETY 159

CHAPTER XXII
FUNDAMENTAL CONCLUSIONS 168

GLOSSARY 170

CHAPTER I

THE RATIONAL ATTITUDE

MANY years ago I was amused by hearing a rhetorical, rather than an exact, clergyman tell his congregation: " Sin is like a serpent; the serpent looks at the bird and fascinates it till it can move neither *hand* nor *foot*!"

Putting on one side the question of the anatomical construction of a bird, the notion that snakes fascinate the frogs, little birds, and so on, that they catch and devour, is ill-founded. Extreme fright is often caused and most of the victims rush about madly, are by no means catalepsed. Moreover, a person who is paralysed by an oncoming motor is not fascinated by it.

However, as a contrast to behaviours of that kind, may be added an incident connected with myself. It occurred when during the spring of 1935 I was making a practical study, at Whipsnade Zoological Gardens, of certain aspects of animal psychology. I was spotted by a journalist. He at once jumped to the conclusion that I was trying to hypnotise some of the animals. I told him that such was not my object, and, indeed, that in view of the real nature of hypnotism, I could not accept the claim of individuals who professed to be able to perform that feat. " Animals," I said, " can be rendered, on occasion, more docile or fearful by means of gaze, and certain birds can be made to fall asleep by moving a finger round and round their heads; moreover, by ingenious expedients, fowl may be made cataleptic—rigid; but not one of those occurrences is hypnotism in the true sense. The fascination exercised on some animals by music may be considered to have some sort of connection with hypnotism, for both are concerned with contemplation. However," I jocularly added, "if I could get indisputable evidence that I had made a monkey more efficient in mental arithmetic, I might have some solid grounds from which to conclude that I had managed to hypnotise him." The journalist did not call in question the accuracy of my remark, but, from the expression on his face, he seemed to think he had been surreptitiously robbed of his "story." It happened, however, that whilst I was looking at a zebra in which I was considerably interested, the animal seemed to shy, kicked up his heels, and galloped to his paddock. From thence, according to the account that ultimately appeared in the *Sunday Graphic*, the zebra watched me "reproachfully for half-an-hour." Referring to that legend, and apparently some incidents with other animals (certainly not with the vast majority), the newspaper account stated: "There must be something in his piercing brown eyes that affects them."

Julius Cæsar said: "People readily believe what they wish to be true;" and Charles II, "the Merry Monarch," explained the success of a then popular preacher with his congregation by saying: "His nonsense suits their nonsense." The explanation certainly applies to the avidity with which superstitious and fantastic notions are often swallowed without question. A few years ago a public test of the fire-walking usually accepted as fact, yielded the result that common-sense would have supposed—that the Indian's feet were burned, as were those of British volunteers who accompanied him upon his journey. Instead of any leisurely sauntering through the heated charcoal, the passage took about two seconds! Think now of levitation, and of how a fashionable audience was induced by a Harley Street specialist to " witness " how it was produced. The perhaps hypnotised person raised her arms and legs, but still lay on the ground. As I remarked in the *Daily Mail*, were levitation a fact, the law of gravitation would be non-existent, and weights-and-measures men would be out of business. Since then, an offer of £500 put forth by me did not lead to substantiation of levitation, nor to any attempt to substantiate it. A like result followed an offer made by the Magic Circle.

In my book on *Personality: Its Nature, Its Operation and Its Development* I wrote a chapter entitled: " Truth about the Yogis." Therein I remarked: " Periods of time and periods of space would seem to bestow, in the estimation of some minds, distinction and even a special right to credence; but inasmuch as it is not always an easy matter to test the truth of claims made near at hand, it surely behoves everyone to be chary of adopting views the ground of which cannot be tested without difficulty—and perhaps not at all." During my professional tour in India (1949), " periods of space " were very greatly shortened though not entirely abolished, but I did not discover anything that was contrary to the views I expressed previously regarding Yoga.

One might extend much further a relation of pseudo-scientific wonders, but that is unnecessary. My published books show that I am no mystery-monger. The experiments made by me throughout the first decade of this century solved, in the estimation of many reputable scientists, the much-vexed question of the actual nature of the mental condition utilised in hypnotism. Victor Neuburg declared that he was not going beyond the truth in asserting that I found hypnotism a superstition and made of it a science. Nevertheless, it is a lamentable fact that, as deplored by Professor R. J. Berry regarding ostensible psychology, there is much " sloppy thinking " prevalent in his own —the medical—profession. The truth of that indictment may I think be gauged correctly from extracts from letters written to me a few years ago by a justly-celebrated alienist, Dr. W. Reid McGlashan, Physician to the Mental Health Services, States of Guernsey. " Until I read your books the theory of Hypnotism appeared so insulting to my reason that I did not take the trouble to investigate what, even if it was doing any good, seemed to be bluff and bunkum; your theory and explanations convince me that hypnotism is a rational reality, and if the operator be convinced he is likely to do more good than an operator who blunders along with something that appears a shadow and a sham." Later, Dr. McGlashan generously wrote to me: " I wish to assure you that whatever expression of mine may seem to you useful in the interests of truth regarding the subject of Hypnotism is at your service to reproduce whenever and wherever you may deem it appropriate." Since writing the two letters from which I have quoted, Dr. McGlashan has written the Foreword to my book, *Emile Coué: The Man and his Work*. Therein he kindly states: "As an eminently successful exponent and practitioner of Hypnotism (as it really is and not as it is frequently fancied to be) the author merits the gratitude of thousands of thinkers, in addition to that of many more thousands of alleviated sufferers. . . . He has dragged from the dark a doctrine and a method of healing which has too long been hidden in the murk and mist of metaphysics, or worse still, in the slough of superstition."

More than half a century has elapsed since Moll, a famous Berlin physician and hypnotist, stated: "Hypnotism is a mine for the psychological investigator, for hypnosis is nothing but a mental state."

Personally, I have no hesitation in affirming that the truths underlying what is genuine in hypnotism are an *essential* part of psychology. By deft contrivances hypnotism reveals hitherto latent abilities, makes something that has been abnormal to all but a few "gifted" individuals normal to many individuals supposed to be mediocre or even obtuse. I would emphasise without delay the fact that when minds are working inexpertly, the results of so-called "intelligence tests" are unreliable. It is with the mental, as with the vocal, the study of voice-production is but a means towards an end, not the end itself.

CHAPTER II

SOME PERTINENT HISTORICAL FACTS

ALTHOUGH little more than a century has elapsed since the word " hypnotism " was first used, the history of the art underlying the science extends to very ancient times, there being ample reasons for concluding that the art—in a rather crude form—was practised by the Ancient Egyptians, the Syrians, Chaldeans, Babylonians, Hebrews, Indians, Chinese, Greeks and Romans.

Much of the early history of hypnotism is bound up with Egyptian religions, with the ceremonies of crystal gazing, and of treatments by laying-on of hands, with utterances of the great Greek oracles, with some of the most sacred Oriental mysteries, and with the confusion of the abnormal with the miraculous during the Middle Ages. The history of hypnotism strikingly illustrates throughout the fact that, though doubtless " knowledge is power," some good use may be made of an *art* while yet the corresponding *science* is in its infancy.

The word " hypnotism " is derived from a Greek word meaning " sleep," and was coined by the surgeon, James Braid, who, on the 29th June, 1842, read before the British Association at Manchester, where he practised, a paper entitled " A Practical Essay on the Curative Agency of Neuro-Hypnotism " (" nervous sleep "). Braid's attention had been drawn to the matter through demonstrations, given in this country in 1841, by La Fontaine, a French "mesmerist" or "magnetist." One of this operator's performances in Manchester was attended by Braid and a fellow practitioner, with the intention of putting an end to what they considered "a humbug." The two doctors stepped on to the platform to make a public exposure, but found that on vitally important points they themselves were deluded. Nevertheless, Braid was not completely satisfied, and therefore attempted (and in part succeeded) in putting upon a basis consistent with well-established physiological facts what had been mixed up with spurious phenomena and far-fetched theories. The name "hypnotism" was consistent with his early conclusions. He later attempted, but unsuccessfully, to substitute "monoideism" for "hypnotism," saying that a hypnotic condition was never more than apparently one of sleep, and that the results were due mainly to being engrossed with a single idea. In reality the terms were equally misleading.

Nowadays the words "hypnotism" and "mesmerism" are practically synonymous. Mesmerism took its name from Friedrich (or Franz) Anton Mesmer (1733-1815), who apparently believed that a healing force lay in himself—that, indeed, it pervaded the whole universe and affected the nervous systems of men. When, in 1778 Mesmer held séances in Paris, the city was thrown into a state of great excitement by the remedial results of his art. His séances were thronged by persons of all classes. However, a Commission of Inquiry, appointed by the French Academy of Sciences in 1784, ascribed such results as did occur to imagination.

Mesmer called his hypothetical, invisible and undiscoverable fluid " animal magnetism." A theory almost identical with his was promulgated, as early as 1679, by William Maxwell, a Scot. The word " magnetism " was, however, somewhat similarly used by Theophrastus Bombastus von Hoenheim (1493-1541), better known under his assumed name, Paracelsus. However, *since* Mesmer explanatory theories similar to his have been propounded. Such was Baron Reichenbach's theory of " odyle." In 1850, two American lecturers introduced what they called " electro-biology," stating that the results were due to generating electric currents in the bodies of persons upon whom they operated. If hypnotic adaptability were proportionate to the capacity of giving electric shocks, the electric eel would be a superb operator! In reality, anyone can give a slight electric shock by shuffling the feet on a carpet during clear, cold weather, and then touching some especially sensitive spot on another person—nose, ear or (and better still) tongue.

Many facts (particularly the possibility of self-hypnotism) show the fallacy of the mesmeric and allied theories.

Braid originally thought that the principal agent whereby the hypnotic condition (technically called "hypnosis") was induced was the staring he advocated; but he later modified his views on that matter, ascribing most of the effect to " suggestion "—*i.e.*, to the influence of ideas.

There was a definite similarity between the later beliefs of Braid, and those of Dr. W. B. Fahnestock, a Chicago medical man who, since he held that the phenomena evinced were due to the unimpeded action of the *subject's own mind,* called the condition "statuvolism"—from the Latin "status" (" a state ") and " volo " (" I will ").

Extending Braid's early principle, later operators have employed fatiguing the senses of hearing and touch. The famous neurologist, Charcot (of the Salpêtrière Hospital, Paris) sometimes used forcible means, *e.g.*, sudden and strong flashes of light. Unfortunately the only class of persons he experimented upon habitually were admittedly hysterical. In contradistinction to the Salpêtrière School was the Nancy School founded by Antoine Liébault, a doctor, who worked philanthropically for many years, and Professor Hypolité Bernheim, his convert and pupil. Liébault and Bernheim supposed that the hypnotic condition was sometimes sleep and sometimes a condition approximating to it. (I shall show later why that contention does not hold water.) Bernheim declared : " The whole system of magnetic medicine is only the medicine of the imagination; the imagination is put into such a condition by the hypnosis that it cannot escape from the suggestion." I should say at once that the mere fact that Bernheim's own " subjects " would sometimes refuse, even from caprice, to obey his suggestions disproves his theory.

At the present day, persons who follow in the main the methods of the Nancy School hold very modified theories. Procedures, too, have been varied and modified considerably; and, in connection with certain theories and the practice of Emile Coué, there came into existence what is sometimes termed "The Second Nancy School." Putting on one side the stories which introduce the reputed " rope trick " and other wonders, Coué was the first operator whose name was particularly associated with mass-hypnotism—camouflaged by him as " auto-suggestion." After dealing with sufferers individually, he was accustomed to give collective suggestion, and, during that procedure, many of the " class " passed into a condition of hypnosis, not infrequently of a profound nature. As misstatements on that and other matters have been commonly made by friends, as well as foes, of Coué, I venture to refer my readers, for further particulars, to my book, *Emile Coué: The Man and his Work.*

My own contributions to the theory of hypnotism will be dealt with in future chapters of the present work.

CHAPTER III

WHAT HYPNOTISM IS NOT

When, in the year 1901, I personally took up the practical investigation of hypnotism and its phenomena, I had, of course, to commence with a working hypothesis, but a host of hypotheses existed from which to choose. Hypnotism was most commonly viewed as the art and science of inducing and using a condition (*hypnosis*) characterised by increased suggestibility—*i.e.*, with proneness on the part of the " subject " to accept as true, and to act in accordance with, ideas presented by the operator. Some who held that opinion declared that hypnotic processes induced sleep or a tendency thereto. Others denied the justice of that contention; and some went so far as to deny that increased suggestibility was in any way characteristic of the hypnotic state. As a working hypothesis I assumed that hypnotic procedure induced sleep or a tendency to it, and that hypnotic " somnambulism " corresponded to ordinary sleep-walking—modified.

Sleep is somewhat of a mystery and admits of various degrees of intensity. Possibly there is dreamless slumber, complete oblivion, but that is questionable. Most dreams are merely *thought*, but there may be talking during sleep, there may be trivial actions, but there may also be walking, combined with partial observation. Among dreamers, some are accustomed to carry out, when asleep, intricate mental work, accompanied by some physical; but when all the senses are in action a person is no longer sleeping. Lapses of the power to recollect can readily—too readily—be taken as evidence of sleep having occurred; such lapses sometimes occur through fatigue or debility. Moreover, there is a pathological condition known as "day-time somnambulism," one characteristic of which is profound lapse of memory.

Hypnosis varies in intensity, and it is unquestionable that a person may pass from definite hypnosis to sound slumber. Drowsiness, for a particular reason which I shall mention later, is of service in connection with hypnosis, but it is not essential. By the way, I have known persons with whom I was hypnotically experimenting to become fast asleep and to be awakened a moment later, and unintentionally, by the sound of my voice. Such persons have told me that I awoke them in the middle of a dream.

Not long elapsed after I commenced my investigation of hypnotism before I perceived the fallacy of attempting to identify hypnosis with any condition of sleep. Whoever entertains the notion that hypnosis is ordinary sleep, or extraordinary sleep, modified by suggestions, should reflect upon the fact that were the assumptions made in dreams believed afterwards, disastrous results would inevitably occur—we should be insane! That consideration is sufficient to discredit the notion that belief is equally powerful whatever the mental condition may happen to be during which it occurs.

What led to and supported the notion that deep hypnosis is identical with sleep? In the first place, the lapse of recollection that sometimes—not always—occurs regarding the events of hypnosis. Secondly, the word "sleep" is often employed by the operator, who may suppose (though during hypnosis his subjects certainly do not) that the suggestion has been literally actualised. Thirdly, attributed acted-dreams, whence deeply hypnotised persons in an alert condition are sometimes termed "somnambules." Fourthly, the supposed credulity manifested by the subject of the experiment.

As regards lapse of the ability to recollect, it is an everyday occurrence in ordinary life—as, for example, when a required name is forgotten. In reality, after hypnosis there may be lucid recollection; and in any case an appropriate suggestion is almost certain to ensure remembrance when desired.

Why do hypnotised persons act ridiculously on the stage? The answer to this question dispenses with the third and fourth reasons given regarding the supposed identity of sleep and deep hypnosis, and also throws a flood of light on other errors regarding hypnotism.

Some stage-subjects supposed to be hypnotised are nothing of the kind; indeed, it is no uncommon thing for an ostensibly hypnotic demonstration so to combine the false and the true that onlookers disagree among themselves as to the genuineness of the performance, and not only do they attend again to satisfy themselves, but the curiosity of persons who hear the dispute is often so aroused that they too attend. Nevertheless, among genuinely hypnotised persons (on and off the stage) are those who purposely simulate (and may be paid for so doing), some who imagine themselves dominated up to a point (because that has been their conception of hypnotism), and others because they are very "suggestible," by which is meant that they readily fall in with views expressed, are credulous and over obliging. Such are the persons who, under the fire of a brisk and insinuating cross-examination in a law-court, are readily led into assenting to, and even into making, false statements. Hypnotism does not at once prevent persons of this type from displaying their unfortunate propensity, though by degrees it may entirely dissipate it for very good reasons which will become apparent to any intelligent person who reflects upon the contents of my chapter dealing with what hypnotism really is. But the fact should be clear at once that one reason why there has been so much confusion as regards the nature of hypnotism is that insufficient attention has been given to the characteristics of subjects previous to hypnotisation, which explains why a pronounced tendency to credulity and obedience has commonly been looked upon as a symptom of hypnosis. Nevertheless, inconsistent with that view of hypnotism, the investigators concerned have omitted to guard adequately against the acceptance of spurious phenomena as genuine. That omission caused me early to suspect, and later to be sure, that some accredited authorities on hypnotism drew their conclusions from experimenting with a few suggestible persons—and no one else. The only phenomena of which very suggestible persons seem to have a monopoly are *unverifiable*—which, considering the nature of the matter, is almost equivalent to saying that the phenomena in question are non-existent. In reality, though all sane persons may benefit from hypnotism, the finest effects are induced in (and one can also say " by ") the most intelligent persons. Surely, that is as one should expect, the results being bound up with thought.

A small minority of persons can, in " normal " life, conjure up what, with the addition of belief, would be visual hallucinations and illusions. Hypnotism tends to increase that ability, and can induce and develop it in many persons. Hallucinations and illusions (of sight and hearing) of such a nature as to constitute delusions, are not hypnotic phenomena—although, of course, a person prone to hallucinations and illusions (for example, a morphinomaniac whom I treated) may experience them at a time when it so happens he is hypnotised.

From a superficial observation of stage " expositions " of hypnotism, and, unfortunately, the observations of some reputed psychologists, when a stick is put into a " subject's " hands, and he treats it as a serpent in accordance with the operator's statement that it is one, the " subject " ceases to see the stick, but, instead, an imaginary serpent, occupying the same position as the stick. If that were actually the case, the stick would be a nonentity to the " subject ";

but, in reality, he realises both its position and dimensions. Moreover, if the stick be taken away from the " subject," but he be told that he is still handling the serpent, before acting in accordance with that suggestion he must realise the absence of the stick from his hands. Whoever assumes that hypnotised persons, when carrying out ridiculous suggestions, are completely deluded, loses sight of the fact that these persons are simultaneously discriminating as to how they can best imitate. The fact is therefore clear that when "subjects" act parts during hypnosis, they are not completely deluded; they feel those parts, like actors, but, underneath everything, they *know* they are not the persons they represent. Naturally, therefore, even the most suggestible subjects refuse, at times, to comply with commonplace, to say nothing of repugnant suggestions. That suffices to show that by hypnotism persons are deprived of neither intelligence, nor initiative. On the contrary, as I shall show later, hypnotic procedures tend to develop a commonly neglected side of the mentality—the meditative.

When taking into consideration the foregoing explanation, what importance can rightly be ascribed to the *mock* crimes adduced—with the excuse that actual crimes are unlawful—by certain operators as evidence that their subjects are mere puppets in their fingers? Inasmuch as the tests are founded on the suppositions that increase of credulity is the key to hypnotism and that the ascribed hallucinations and illusions are *absolutely* genuine, assassinations with cardboard daggers, and such-like pseudo-criminal acts, are surely valueless as tests. It is a most significant fact that in the French hospitals the " best subjects " would go to the highest bidder. No wonder that it does not appear that any experimenter has succeeded in leading a hypnotee to reveal the inner work of Freemasons or Hibernians!

More will be written on this matter in my seventh chapter.

At a meeting of the British Association on 3rd September, 1937, Dr. William Brown, it seems, " explained " that hypnotism is a mental condition during which the subject is unable to see a sixth person in a room if told that there are only five. How, then, does Dr. Brown's advocacy of *self*-hypnotism stand? Tacitly, we are asked to believe that a person mentally so affected is in a fit condition to formulate and give suggestive treatment to himself or herself! Dr. Brown's inconsistency was an outcome of adducing as a symptom of hypnosis what is but a personal characteristic—*viz.*, extreme suggestibility. He assumed that assent to a suggestion implies actualisation also.

Braid, who, it will be remembered, coined the term " hypnotism," declared that his subjects were not puppets; and a like assertion was made by Fahnestock still earlier. So far as I was concerned, as Prof. Delbœuf and Dr. Milne Bramwell (two first-class hypnotists) also admitted regarding themselves, the recognition of the independence of the subject was forced upon me, despite preliminary assumption to the contrary, by constantly recurring experiences.

In concluding this chapter, a few words should be said regarding phenomena that appear because expected by subjects. The supposed "rapport" between operator and subject is purely artificial—indeed, there need be no operator other than the subject himself. There are no real "stages" of hypnosis—stages to be determined in accordance with the phenomena that appear—although there are degrees of intensity of the condition. As to anæsthesia, it rarely appears without preliminary expectation on the part of the subject.

Is hypnotism, then, solely a matter of suggestion? Not so. With the joint object of dissipating repugnance and of instilling confidence, it is the custom of many operators to give each of their subjects an opportunity of witnessing the hypnotisation of someone else. As a further assistance, a description is also vouchsafed of what the *operator contends* is hypnosis. "Here, then," someone is likely to exclaim, "is a clear evidence that *expectation* is the key to hypnotism!" But in reality—although effects of expectation are often clearly discernible—the adduced circumstance points to an exactly contrary conclusion. Despite the clashing of theories, a like ground-work (hypnosis) is induced; and, therefore, it is evident that each of the varying sets of hypnotic processes has, *in itself, a definite and similar* value. The consideration of what that value is I must leave for a future chapter.

CHAPTER IV

THE "PHYSICAL" AND THE "MENTAL."

"WHAT is Matter?" asked *Punch*, and answered, "Never mind." "What is Mind?" "Never matter.' Personally, I should say, "Mind, it *does* matter."

A lecturer began to address his audience thus: "What is Mind?—Nobody knows. We only know the *manifestations* of mind."

The lecturer might have said just as truly: "What is Matter?—Nobody knows. We know only the *manifestations* of matter."

What do we know except through manifestations? The physicist may show that all matter is made up of "atoms," and that an atom is made up of electrons moving round and round a nucleus or proton. Further, taking advantage of this fact, he may so disturb the movements of the electrons as to realise, in a measure, the dreams of the alchemists, by turning quicksilver into gold. Nevertheless, though he may show that in the final analysis all matter has a single basis, he cannot know what matter really is—his experience is with but *symbols*.

For example, if an object appears red, that colour is but an idea and merely signifies that the object has absorbed the remaining primary rays of light—*viz.*, what amount in effect to blue and yellow.

In other words, the colour is that in the object which causes in persons with normal eyes the sensation ordinarily experienced—which, in that instance, may be described as " a red sensation."

The Brahmans teach that " Nothing exists but one Universal Spirit called 'Brahman,' and whatever appears to exist separate from that spirit is mere illusion." Various mystics, notably Mrs. Eddy (the founder of the spurious science called " Christian Science "), have made a like contention. " Tumours, ulcers, inflammation, pain, deformed spines, are all dream shadows," confidently affirmed the lady referred to. She died, notwithstanding—of a dream shadow (of course), death being an illusion! Indeed, of dream shadows, either in our own minds, or in those of the victims, the imaginary bodies of—should I say " imaginary?"—creatures lower in the scale than ourselves are continually appearing to die.

In truth the reality of a world external to our consciousness, and consequently the reality of matter, is impossible of genuine disbelief—is a primary truth which must be assumed before arguing or any other mode of voluntary mental activity can commence.

One is unable to think of consciousness apart from a something (actual or imaginary) to which the consciousness is ascribed.

Though in ordinary parlance we talk of *mental* causes in contradistinction to *physical* ones, when we attempt to analyse the nature of a so-called " mental " cause we find ourselves unable to represent it in thought without taking into account a physical basis, whether the origin be external or internal.

Many philosophers have been puzzled to explain why, when we will to move a limb, we think of the end desired, and not of the means, though doubtless between the volition and the result there occur nervous impulses leading to the requisite muscular contractions.

If we look upon thought as purely abstract, we cannot take a step towards explaining; but if we look upon the volition as corresponding to the first of the chain of *physical* causes, the question assumes a very different aspect; and that is the view taken for granted by all serious physiologists and psychologists.

Much is said of the soothing (and other) effects of music "on the mind." However, there have to be taken into account the physical organs of hearing, and a certain portion of the brain where auditory impressions are registered—the destruction of which portion (as proved by experiment and pathology) makes the auditory impressions of no effect.

Though it is customary to speak of the effects of emotions "on the body," if we look closely at an emotion and try to get in our consciousness a clear picture of it, we find that we are forced to take into account various physical peculiarities which are bound up with it, the bodily symptoms of an emotion being as truly tied to the feeling in consciousness as the movement of a limb is tied to the thought from which it arises. King Louis XVI was correct when he protested: "I am not afraid; feel my pulse."

So much for " mental " causes. As " physical " agents, think of the effects of chloroform, of alcohol, of tea and coffee, and so on. Why have those agents their known effects on the mental power? Merely because the brain changes correspond to the mental.

Throughout the organism, functional activity is accompanied by a flow to the part exercised of nerve energy, and, following upon that, of blood; conversely, when the blood supply to any part of the organism has decreased we can be assured that the part is resting—partially or completely. As regards rest and functional activity, the brain conforms to the same laws as does the rest of one's organism: during profound slumber the brain is partially deprived of blood, whereas during vigorous mental labour it is well supplied with it.

Whatever affects the brain affects the mind, and the extent of the influence of the mind is dependent on the condition of the physical organism as a whole and also as a collection of parts.

Development of brain and degree of intelligence vary in accordance with species of animals, races of mankind, and individual humans.

If, using both eyes, we look at an object, we are really viewing it from two positions, though, in persons with normal eyes, the mental picture is not exactly like either reflection, but a combination and blending of the two. The cinematograph is another illustration—one that forcefully illustrates the fact that *duration* concerns consciousness. Every conscious thought takes up an appreciable time, and any nervous process of lesser duration is necessarily unconscious to the individual.

Consciousness, as we know it, appears to be a *condition*, and this due to centralisation of the nervous system. For every thought of which we *as individuals* are conscious, there are *many nervous* processes; and a child at birth has no thoughts, only the capacity of acquiring them. The acquirement results from stimulation, external and internal, in the first place; later, also from action and reaction between the stored-up impressions. Much mental work is performed of which we are not conscious *as individuals*, whilst it is occurring, though we may know of the result later. True education so establishes associations of ideas and actions that much of what we wish to do becomes automatic, and, consequently, during its performance we can attend to other things. Walking, writing, reading, playing a musical instrument, typewriting, cycling, and even swimming, are all cases in point. But more: the brain can carry out intricate mental work to which attention is not being given consciously. This function has been called " unconscious cerebration."

It is important that the fact be realised that there is a mental selective and inventive power in addition to whatever is conscious to us. Were that not the case one could not even sort out and arrange ideas; whereas the intelligence at the back of what is conscious can arrange material for lectures or books, and often solves baffling mental problems. It often happens that what one accepts at first because not contrary to ideas " near consciousness " is afterwards seen to be wrong, the adverse judgment coming suddenly into consciousness from " unconscious cerebration." Unless comparisons and judgments were made below consciousness this could not happen. If, however, with some writers, we apply the word " consciousness " to this background, we must not only carefully distinguish the empirical consciousness from that which is hypothetical, we must assume the existence of an infinite number of consciousnesses in connection with each person. Further, if we assume that consciousness is merely the inner side of a nervous process, we must ascribe it to a child prior to birth, to even dead persons for a little time, and to every cell in the human body. Consciousness, as we know it, gives the expression to the face; or, rather, the expression corresponds in a way to what is conscious. Division, or disassociation, of consciousness does not show that another *mind* has been entered, though it often does occur in connection with a *modification of the form taken by consciousness.*

Persons may be in real agreement as to matter-of-fact and yet employ different terms; and others may use like terms, but differ as to matter-of-fact. Some writers prefer to restrict the employment of the word " mind " to consciousness, and to speak of the other " mental " processes in physiological terms only. Personally, by " mind " I mean the sum-total of one's mental experience—everything of which one has been conscious, and of which there is a record of some kind left in one's organism—a record which can, and often does, influence one's present—and may influence one's future—thoughts, feelings and decisions. Consciousness is in a way comparable to a sheet upon which pictures may be thrown by two magic lanterns, one on each side of it; for ideas that appear "in consciousness" may enter through the organs of sensation or from mind unconscious to the individual.

In the light of the foregoing observations, how should mind be viewed in relation to matter, the *mental* to the *physical*? The ascertainable facts do not seem to justify the statement that man is made up of two distinct entities; and that great physiologist and anthropologist, Professor Sir Arthur Keith, has written, with equal courage and frankness: "I know of no one who has inquired at first hand into the human brain and has been able thereafter to believe in any form of dualism." Without claiming that any part of the world other than living organisms is conscious, it seems probable that what is at present not part of mind may nevertheless at some future time become conscious inasmuch as it may be taken up by an organism endowed with requisite brain and nervous systems. It would seem as correct to describe the universe as made up of "mind-stuff" or "psychic-stuff," as, verbally, to give the preponderance to the physical aspect. In any case, the relevant facts seem to substantiate the description given to Man by Professor Alexander Bain, *viz.*, "a double-faced unity." It should therefore be understood that, although certain causes may be described legitimately as "mental" and others as "physical," when I make that differentiation it is solely for the sake of clearness and convenience.

CHAPTER V

WHAT HYPNOTISM IS

In his *Life of Frederick the Great,* Thomas Carlyle declared genius to be " the transcendent capacity for taking trouble first of all," and elsewhere as " an infinite capacity for taking pains." A correspondent of *The Daily Mail* inquired as to whether, on the contrary, genius is not the capacity of doing a thing infinitely well *without* taking infinite pains.

When Sir Isaac Newton was asked how he had achieved his discoveries, he replied: " By always intending my mind." " Intention " (may I remark?) was formerly used to imply a fixed direction of the mind to a particular object, or in a particular way. As regards its opposite, even the great philosopher, John Locke, could write (in his work on *The Conduct of the Understanding*): " A proper and effectual remedy for this wandering of thoughts I would be glad to find. He that shall propose such an one would do great service to the studious and contemplative part of mankind, and perhaps help unthinking men to become thinking." And coming to the year 1839, Isaac D'Israeli, the father of the famous politician, wrote in his book, *On the Literary Character*: " A work on the art of meditation has not yet been produced. . . . We may suspect, since men of genius in the present age have confided to us the secrets of their studies, that this art may be carried on by more obvious means than at first would appear, and even by mechanical contrivances and practical habits. A mind well organised may be regulated by a single contrivance, as by a bit of lead we govern the fine machinery by which we track the flight of time. Many secrets in this art of the mind yet remain as insulated facts, which may hereafter enter into an experimental history."

The word *genius* is derived from a Greek word meaning "to beget," and originally signified the original structure and bent of one's mind. However some of the ancients, assuming that a good or evil spirit or demon, presided over each individual's destiny in life (directing his or her birth and conduct, and acting as guide), the word *genius* was applied to that personification of inherent characteristics and conduct. Gradually, the signification became restricted to such persons as were enabled and led by their "familiar spirits" to display extraordinary mental capacity. Lastly, instead of being the mouthpiece of a genius, the individual was called a genius.

The expressed feeling of one genius speaks for every genius: "There is a fatality in the first chance which suggests your idea," said a great writer, Goncourt. "Then there is an *unknown force*, a *superior will*, a sort of necessity of writing which commands your work and guides your pen; so much so that sometimes the book which leaves your hands does not seem to have come out of yourself; it astonishes you, like something which was in you, and of which you were unconscious." Whence came the ideas in reality? They were results of brain-work unconscious to the individual as an individual. Why came they? Because trains of thought had been begun during meditation, had been continued by unconscious brain-work, and their results were allowed to become conscious during another meditative mood—whereas effort would have led to diversion, would have thwarted.

Sometimes a genius may baffle himself. Leonardo da Vinci, who, it should be borne in mind, was not only an artist, but an engineer and a man of remarkable scientific attainments, when brought to a stand through lack of serviceable ideas, would stare into a heap of ashes. Almost isolated in thought from his surroundings, his imagination would not be hampered, and in a " brown study " there would come into his consciousness just what he wanted. The philosopher, Moses Mendelssohn (grandfather of the composer), when he reached a point of difficulty, would go to his window and count the tiles on his neighbour's house-top.

The recognition of the enormous intellectual value of meditation led the Greek orator, Demosthenes, to pursue his studies for months together in a subterranean chamber; and Democritus, a Greek philosopher, blinded himself in order to facilitate meditation. Darkening of their apartments was resorted to by Malebranche, Hobbes, Corneille and others. John Stuart Mill, when in Parliament, rather than present an argument unskilfully would close his eyes and remain silent for two or three minutes at a time if necessary. His auditors thought themselves well compensated for the delay. Hoffman would often say to his friends: " When I wish to compose I sit down to the piano, shut my eyes, and play what I hear." An acquaintance of Sir Isaac Newton stated of that philosopher: "He would sometimes be silent and thoughtful, and look all the while as if he were saying his prayers."

As regards the intensity of this contemplative mood, many historical examples might be quoted. Of Socrates it was stated that he was seen by the Athenian army to stand for a whole day and night motionless, with fixed gaze. "And thus," declared Alcibiades, "Socrates is ever wont to do when his mind is occupied with enquiries in which there are difficulties to be overcome. He then never interrupts his meditation, and forgets to eat, to drink, and sleep—everything, in short, until his enquiry has reached its termination, or, at least, until he has seen some light in it." Archimedes was meditating in his bath when he discovered his famous "hydrostatic principle" and in the same mental condition he appeared nude in public, having forgotten to put on his clothes. During another meditation he received his death-wound, being unaware until that moment of the storming of Syracuse, his city. Of the Italian poet, Marino, it is related that he was so absorbed in a composition that for some time he was insensible to the burning of a leg. However, I emphatically decline to vouch for the veracity of the anecdote told of a professor (name unknown) who, upon returning home one night, put his umbrella in his bed and then stood in the corner!

I hope that I have made the point clear that although a conspicuous peculiarity of genius is what is called "absence of mind," the use made of that mental condition is sometimes far more unique than "wool-gathering." No genius is without special aptitudes, which form the predisposition, but without the right attitude of mind, and continued attention, genius cannot develop. An old Roman writer (Plautus) exclaimed: "How oft the greatest genius lies concealed!"

In passing, it may be of use to refer to a notion held by some persons that genius is in some way allied to madness. Such persons should take to heart this statement of a conspicuously level-headed, as well as brilliant, man, the late Sir Frederick Mott, who equally distinguished himself in pathology and neurology and was a physician to King George the Fifth: "It is a great mistake to suppose that a stock which does not show pathological mental instability in the form of epilepsy or insanity cannot therefore produce genius."

When a person's character is looked at very closely, there are likely to be revealed peculiarities that pains have been taken to conceal. That is equally the case when a person is born "important" or becomes so. In a conspicuously clever person, these peculiarities are likely to be somewhat different from what are observed in mediocre or dull persons. A conspicuously able person is less affected by custom than are most people, and therefore is somewhat like an odd man in a box of tin soldiers.

For a few moments let us now consider some kinds of physical aptitude. There is a proverb of the Jesuits which runs: "What you wish to do quickly, set about slowly." It is a rule of very wide application. Take.

for example, pianoforte playing. The incompetent teacher of the pianoforte commonly leaves his or her pupils to acquire facility of fingering by means of much practice, not realising that an action is never easy when opposed by wrong or unnecessary muscular contraction. Against that haphazard method (or rather, lack of method) let me place the method advocated by *expert* teachers of the pianoforte. *They* say to the pupil: "Relax the muscles of your wrist and fingers, merely letting the hand rest upon the keys, in such and such a position. Then, without making any part of the hand in the least rigid, lift the finger or fingers required." By this expedient the pupil learns the desired "knack," and, as a consequence, a fine technique can readily be acquired—a technique otherwise rarely even approached.

It is much the same with the skilled athlete, whose strength appears phenomenal, as with the skilled pianist, the "knack" here consisting of bringing into play the muscles required and suppressing the action of those which would hinder or prevent success. And how does the athlete attain this necessary isolation of muscle action? Like the pianist, by first going as nearly as possible to the other extreme—by commencing with muscular *relaxation*.

Before public audiences I have demonstrated hundreds of times that the ordinary man is enormously stronger physically than he has supposed himself to be; and I have also demonstrated that he is enormously stronger mentally, too. In short, I have shown wherein the thought of the genius differs essentially from that of the supposedly normal man. How have I done this? By means of hypnotic procedures.

Please to reflect that the procedures termed, inclusively, "hypnotic," and what were deemed, rightly or wrongly, to be their results, were empirical in the first place, and that conjecture and inefficient observation each played a part. Repetition of what had seemed to prove effective occurred without clear and correct notions of the comparative values or uselessness of procedures. Accretions, often useless and sometimes hindering or thwarting, were bound up with what was actually effective. Supposing hypnotic procedures, as such, had never come into existence at a time when a desire had existed to increase, as effectively as possible, the capacity of attention, rendering it easy and at the same time profound, what procedure would have been most suitable for the attainment of that object? Surely, the same kind of training should have been adopted here as elsewhere; attempts would, or should, have been made to induce a condition of mental relaxation, and to build, gradually, upon that relaxation a habit of mental economy. Attention as ordinarily exhibited is accompanied by nervous and muscular tension. When attention is as it should be, it is easy. And to be easy it must not be hampered by distracting impressions. The secret of mental power is to cultivate the contemplative mood alongside the observative. A typical genius has the contemplative mood out of proportion to the observative; the ordinary person has a preponderance on the other side, and, therefore, in neither case is the mind *completely* developed. In a well-balanced genius both moods have been developed—but even then usually without realising how. That is why genius does not commonly test the effects of attention, or intention, in certain useful directions. Thus, also, especially as the spurious is often confused with the genuine, it transpires that the contemplative mood of genius is unrecognised as identical with the condition known as hypnosis. An increase in the capability of using various mental powers during hypnosis is a peculiarity noticed by all experienced observers. Would not the circumstance be very curious did hypnotic processes induce a condition conspicuously favourable to the exercise of mental power, but nevertheless unexperienced by genius? And yet the circumstance that the Pythia of Delphi and the Sybil of Cumæ were stated to have lost the memory of all they had declared as oracles, was long ago referred to as one evidence of the practice of hypnotism in the ancient world.

Hypnotism, in its ultimate analysis, is seen to be an educational expedient—an expedient by means of which the groundwork essential to the complete development of our powers, physical and mental, is readily laid. It supplies, as hypnosis, the best possible condition for study and for mental, and physical, drill. It tends to form (extemporises, if you like) *balanced* genius.

Hypnotism is the art and science concerned with the systematic (as contrasted with the haphazard) training, development, and utilisation of attention; and hypnosis is an artificially-induced contemplative *mood*.

When the significance of hypnotic processes is described in words, the induction of hypnosis may seem to be a ridiculously easy matter—one certainly not requiring any particular powers of observation and tact. In reality, the lady was justified who said to me: "When you describe hypnotism it seems of no consequence, though really it is most wonderful."

However, it is much the same with hypnotism as with other science. Who, knowing the physics of wireless, is astonished that the results occur? If what is expected does not occur, the initiated person knows that something mechanical is at fault. Further, though extreme wonder may be aroused at the discovery of the pertinent facts, the physicist is aware that they were gradually led up to and could not have been discovered except by someone conversant with previous discoveries. So it was with hypnotism: my solution (in 1910) of the central problem was really such a little step forward that I was surprised that I had not reached it sooner, and that I was apparently its first discoverer. Other scientists (notably Charles Darwin) had all but forestalled me.

In teaching the art, repeated experiments are usually requisite before the student is able thoroughly to grasp the situation; but usually, sooner or later, the knack is caught—though, of course, all do not become equally skilful operators.

As to hypnosis, especially of a pronounced character, there is one important point which I should emphasise before completing this chapter.

Do you think that an imbecile, or even a very dull person, can truly know what the state of *your* mind is? Unless you think yourself a very dull person, you certainly would not answer my question with a serious affirmative. Well, then, how can a mediocre person correctly imagine exactly how a genius feels during profound meditation? Nevertheless, every self-observative person must be aware that at times his own thoughts run easily, whilst at other times he feels comparatively impotent mentally. Now, in the light of the foregoing remarks the fact must be evident that, however one may attempt to *describe* hypnosis, one can convey but a very limited impression by words alone. If I say (as I do) that its essential peculiarity is that it resembles, and in a measure is identical with, the contemplative mood of genius, that indeed may help to get rid of the odium that is attached by some persons to the idea of hypnotism, but, except with a few who have themselves experienced the luxury of intense contemplation, it does not make anyone actually realise what hypnosis is like in itself. To some, indeed, the description can scarcely convey more regarding hypnosis than a map conveys regarding a country. Accurate realisation can come in one way, and in one way only, and that way is through experiencing in oneself the condition. Putting the whole matter in psychological language: One needs to know the mental condition *subjectively* as well as *objectively*.

CHAPTER VI

SUGGESTION AND AUTO-SUGGESTION

SIMS REEVES stated, regarding Macready the actor, that he was accustomed, when about to personify a vicious character, to hire persons to pinch and otherwise torment him. That bears a rather close analogy to the action of those individuals who stick pins in themselves when disposed to laugh at an undesirable time.

It is related that Mrs. Siddons, upon coming from the stage, would spend a little time in studiously laying aside undesirable mannerisms and frames of mind that she had purposely adopted for the personification of this or that character—much as she would divest herself of articles of clothing she had worn. Sir Henry Irving declared that acting the part of Thomas à Becket, in Tennyson's drama, had ennobled him in private life; Irving threw aside the bad, and clung to the good.

Most, if not all, of my readers are aware of a process by which a haunting tune may be got rid of, *viz.*, by humming something else. If the second tune be hummed an excessive number of times, it is likely to be made thereby as haunting as its predecessor. That process bears an analogy to the whistling of a timid boy, when in the dark, to keep his courage up, and to the war-cries and fantastic movements of warriors (so-called civilised, as well as savage), adopted ostensibly in order solely to affright the enemy. All those processes are *auto-* (*i.e.*, " self ") suggestive in character.

Auto-suggestion, in the sense I here attach to the term, consists in the deliberate employment of mental pictures by oneself in order to influence oneself. Thus there are sometimes brought about definite mental and physical changes of momentous import.

The employment of auto-suggestion is of very ancient origin. Probably the first attempts that can be traced were those of the Hindoos. They employed auto-suggestive processes for the attainment, primarily, of what they considered to be moral perfection. The procedures employed by the Hindu holymen or Yogis are bound up with respiratory and other exercises. In their language, however, there is no exact equivalent to our word " air "; what they inhale for life-purposes they call " prana," in their opinion an element to which all other substances in the universe might be finally reduced. The Yogis revel in mystery, but their close study of the operation of respiratory movements on the nervous system and mental organisation, through the heart and lungs, has not been unproductive. Breath-regulation, as prescribed by the Yogis and called by them " pranayama," has definite mental, as well as physical, significances, despite the indirect and unintentional suggestion and the fiction in which it is enshrouded.

Even in very ancient times the custom of auto-suggestion spread far beyond the confines of India. It was propagated in Chaldea, Mesopotamia, Syria and Egypt. Through Phœnician and Egyptian sources the practice passed to Greece, where it was, above all, taught by Pythagoras and other philosophers. From

Greece the art was transmitted to the Latin moralists. Augustine of Hippo-Regius (354-430) related of a Presbyser, named Restitutus, that he could induce in himself a state of seeming insensibility and lie as if dead. Cardanus stated that he could induce in himself a state of " ecstatic insensibility."

Not until recent times has the practice of auto-suggestion been conducted on anything approaching scientific principles. Particular mention should be made of Dr. Coste de Lagrave, a surgeon-major in the French Army, who contributed a paper to the International Hypnotic Congress of 1889 on auto-suggestion. In advocating auto-suggestion with patients, he preferred to preface it by hypnotic suggestion.

Especially since 1921 the word " auto-suggestion " has obtained, in the popular mind, a much extended signification in consequence of the world-wide fame of Coué. Professor McDougall expressed the opinion that Coué made use, in his séances and public demonstrations, of hypnotism! Nobody was more fully aware of that fact than was Coué himself. Almost the first thing he said to me when we first met (which was at Paris, in May, 1922) was: " You use hypnotism; I do too, but I don't say so—I think it is better not."

For mass-suggestion purposes Coué surreptitiously (but with good intent) aimed at obtaining at least a mild degree of hypnosis in those he treated; and at Nancy he habitually sorted out persons whom he described as " unable to help themselves," and employed with them specifically hypnotic processes.

Eventually Coué came more out of his shell. He was fully alive to the fact that more specific hypnotism than that he usually ventured to advocate would eventually gain the ascendancy.

It was my conviction that Coué had successfully introduced the thin end of the wedge, and that the universal recognition, appreciation, and adoption of anti-mystic psychics could follow apace, which led to my acquiescing to his proposal that our names should be associated as joint-authors of a book on practical psychology. Coué had studied and greatly modified his views through his perusal of some of my writings—notably *Rational Hypnotism*, of which he wrote that it was " a masterly examination and exposition of the whole matter." In justice to myself, I am entitled, and in the cause of progress I am constrained, to mention the actual nature of the collaboration that occurred in *Conscious Auto-Suggestion* primarily. I was never a *disciple* of Coué; with the vast majority of psychologists and neurologists, I am convinced that although his *method* fitted a past age " like a glove," any attempt to treat the Couéistic glove as still suitable must not only prove ineffectual, it must seriously damage the estimation formerly inspired by that glove's appearance and usefulness, the hand having grown considerably. Some evidence of that fact is afforded by the number of persons who, after testing simple Couéism (and rarely without having gained therefrom some benefit) have procured the much greater help that hypnotism, rationally employed, can commonly supply.

CHAPTER VII

CAN HYPNOTISM BE A CRIMINAL AGENT?

Early in 1937, strange stories were related regarding the trial, in Moscow, of Bolshevik leaders. It was said that, previous to entering the Court of Judicature, they were subjected to long and frequent "preparation" by hypnotism, and that their evidence was given during a trance. I was asked by *The Daily Dispatch* whether, as a hypnotic practitioner, I considered the stories consistent with psychological fact. In the article that I wrote in consequence, I said:—

"I have, during the last thirty-seven years, given hypnotic treatment to over thirty thousand persons; and I affirm positively that hypnotism cannot be used successfully to extort confessions or to make persons perform criminal acts. I affirm, just as definitely, that hypnotism has sometimes enabled the innocent to be vindicated, and the vicious to be reformed.

"From time to time 'hypnotic influence' is set up as a defence in criminal cases, but that is because of popular misconception regarding hypnotism. In Kansas a man accused of murder was acquitted on the ground that he was hypnotised, but on his death-bed he confessed that he did not even know what hypnotism was, had never witnessed it, and had set up his plea solely in order to prey upon the superstitions of the public. The Supreme Court of Kansas had, however, previously reviewed the case and decided that the man should not have been acquitted, and that there had apparently been a miscarriage of justice.

"Much of the misconception that exists regarding hypnotism is undoubtedly due to novels (notably 'Trilby'), plays and films that have fixed in the minds of a large section of the public a picture of a strong will dominating a weaker one; and have instilled the notion that in real life villains possessed of hypnotic power force weak-willed innocents into sin and crime. I do not make the absurd assertion that a hypnotist is never a bluffer; but I do assert that persons most accustomed to employing bluff are unlikely to be good hypnotists. . . . . .

"Suppose I were asked to force someone by hypnotism to make a 'confession,' what could I do in that direction? Frankly: I could not *force* the subject to do anything. Persons so disposed will lie or steal during hypnosis as well as out of it. *Nevertheless*, confessions may occur as a result of reflection during hypnosis. A boy was brought to me to be cured of thieving. I appealed, during hypnosis, to the better side of the boy, and, after de-hypnotisation, he produced an article which he had stolen from a London store. His father later rewarded him by giving him a sound thrashing!

"My old friend and champion, Dr. Forbes Winslow, when in New York, was professionally engaged in several criminal cases and spent much time in the Tombs prison, where he was given every opportunity of testing hypnotism in relation to the investigation of crime. All New York was talking of a handsome young married woman accused of murdering her mother by giving her arsenic, contained in soup, whilst a guest at her house. By the mother's death the daughter inherited $80,000; and practically everybody believed the accused guilty. After considerable difficulty, Dr. Forbes Winslow obtained her confidence; hypnosis was induced, and latent memories were revived, which established her innocence. Dr. Winslow reported to the Government, and in due course the woman was discharged.

" Despite stories of ' crook hypnotists,' hypnotism cannot assist in making persons ' cat's paws ' for the committal of crime. On rare occasions I have had would-be clients who had the impudence to ask me to assist them, by hypnotism, to attain nefarious ends—some of these persons wished to be made more expert and self-confident, and other persons to be taught how to dominate by means of hypnotism. I admit that the first class could have been assisted had I felt so disposed. As to the second class, they were prone to lose interest when told that hypnotism is not truly a means of domination, but of liberation."

It is noteworthy that my article met with no retort from ostensible believers in hypnotism as a criminal agent.

The confusion that exists between Hypnotism and Suggestion is deplorable. Suggestion, I beg to repeat, from the psychological standpoint, is an attempt to impress one's own or another's mind; it is used in connection with hypnotism, but also apart from it, and, indeed, necessarily affects our beliefs and actions continually. If statements be made to a person who believes he cannot help acting in accordance with them, that person actually does so act or attempt to act, and *no hypnotism is necessary for the purpose,* though, of course, it may happen that the conduct takes place *during* hypnosis.

Hypnotism in itself is absolutely harmless; but notions held regarding it can be otherwise; and if a person believes that he will act foolishly during hypnosis, that conviction affects his behaviour. Evipan, scopolamine, and other drugs are accredited with the capability of making persons tell the truth. Previously sodium amytal was used with the same purpose; but the original user in that connection (Otto C. Lucy) remarked that distilled water could be just as effective if the taker were suitably deceived. May I remind you of the Middle Ages, when belief in witchcraft ("wickedcraft") and the "evil eye" was held by practically all, however learned? Not only did they believe that the devil entered into humans and other animals, and even into insects, but, what is more remarkable, thousands of persons accused of witchcraft pleaded guilty, gave accounts of their bargains with the devil, and reported what he had said, and what they had said —"confessed," despite the facts that their own lives and properties would be forfeited thereby, and their children rendered homeless and probably friendless.

In the Middle Ages, witchcraft was adduced to explain puzzling and spurious occurrences. Nowadays, hypnotism, or what many suppose hypnotism to be, bears the onus. The Russians, as a nation, are, despite their ascribed atheism, very superstitious; and, as hypnotism has long been employed rather extensively in Russia, in the treatment of disease and moral delinquency, no wonder whispers in streets and factories adduced hypnotism in explanation of the Moscow confessions. Whispered gossip is no proof, however. Formerly, confessions that ostensibly emanated from prisoners were used at trials from which the prisoners were absent. The whispered explanation then was that the confessions were obtained by torture. Are we to assume that the authorities who, it had been asserted, would not stand at torture were incapable of putting forth forged confessions? And in the instance under consideration, are we justified in assuming on the authority of gossip, that, because trials have seemingly been delayed excessively, and after the prolonged confinement, prisoners made confessions surprising because, apparently, likely to hurt themselves (though perhaps not), and that are contrary to what has been assumed to be their former characters, hypnotism is the explanation? Sokolnikov, one of the prisoners, it is noteworthy, was described by someone surprised by his confessions, as previously being addicted to " denying, twisting, and turning." We read, too, of the palpable mental struggle of another prisoner, Radek, and of his " strange, forced behaviour "; but why, if he had been made to believe true what he had confessed, and acted automatically? Would not a more likely explanation be his disloyalty to his former associates under the (reported) threats of the killing of his daughter? Assuming the censored accounts to be trustworthy, conceivably the prisoners were led, somehow or other, to "confess" by the promise that thereby discharge, or remission of punishment, would follow their sentences—as in the case of Sokolnikov and Radek seems to have occurred. That promise may account for their demeanour and statements in court.

Ignorance, superstition and prejudice, fostered (as I remarked) by ridiculous stories such as *Trilby*, have obscured the truth about hypnotism, and still stand in the path of its progress; and, more than anything else, mischief has been wrought by the inculcated notion (in other words, *by the suggested idea*) that the hypnotised person is a puppet in the hands of the hypnotist. Hypnosis comes about because the subject complies, however unwittingly it may be, with certain conditions, and an outside operator is not always indispensable. If the subject persists in doing the wrong things—though, perhaps, convinced that they are the right ones, he or she is temporarily unhypnotisable. On the other hand, if the subject does certain other things, which, maybe, *he or she wrongly thinks are preventive of hypnotisation*, hypnosis does occur. A fallacy underlies the statement so often made that persons cannot be hypnotised against their will. Moreover, I would emphasise the fact that, inasmuch as hypnotised persons may decline to act in accordance with suggestions made (and all experienced operators agree on that point), credulity and obedience cannot be the true explanation of cures made by means of hypnotism.

The vital fact is that during hypnosis mind-power is greatly enhanced in certain respects.

By hypnotism and suasion combined, moral reform can often be effected, though all else may have met with dismal failure. The restoration by hypnotism of lost memories has sometimes led to the vindication of the innocent; but hypnotisation is no bar to lying. With the majority of experienced operators, I hold that virtuous persons cannot be led by hypnotism to act in opposition to their consciences. Nevertheless, a person of criminal tastes could be enabled to become—say, a more effective pickpocket.

NOTE.—When, early in June, 1937, I was travelling to America, I came in contact with John G. Iliff, Professor of Economics at San Mateo Junior College, California. He was returning from a second—a six months'—visit to Russia, and consequently was there whilst the political trials were in progress. His outspoken admissions regarding Russian progress in various directions had previously met with some disfavour in the United States, but were confirmed by his second visit. However, as regards the Russian reports of the trials and " confessions," he assured me of his conviction that they were entirely untrustworthy.

POSTSCRIPT (14th October, 1943).—I have left this chapter intact, although some may consider out-of-date those parts relating to the Russian trials, for I feel, very strongly, that those parts can serve more than one purpose still. Admiration for the achievements of the U.S.S.R. is prone to become so extravagant and reckless that an antidote and an emetic are urgently needed. Parts of the film version of Mr. Joseph Davies' *Mission to Moscow* seemed to me to be destitute of verisimilitude. For example : some of the " plotters " might have been schoolboys admitting to having robbed an orchard. Neither sane, nor able, men would, or could, *volunteer* such confessions, and the introduction of hypnotism as an explanation would (I submit) be obvious nonsense to any hypnotic expert.

CHAPTER VIII

WHY THOUGHT KILLS AND CURES

"THE power of the mind over the body" is a mode of expression one often hears. In the light of the contents of my chapter on *The "Physical" and the "Mental,"* intelligent readers will realise why I prefer to speak of "the Power of Thought" as regards bodily functions, thought being, from the physiological standpoint, a bodily function in itself. Thought, it should ever be borne in mind, is not a mere abstract thing, but, in a sense, concrete; to which I might add that, for curative purposes, it can be excellent building material.

A famous mental specialist, Sir Thomas Clouston, admirably summed up the matter in these words : "The brain must be assumed to be not only the most important organ in the body, but its essential organ, for the sake of which all else exists. It is, in fact, the microcosm of the whole organism, its centre and its master. It receives help from every other organ, but it also largely controls the working of each. By its mental action alone it can hurry the heart's beat or slow its pace; it can make the skin shrivel or flush, it can quicken or stop the digestion, it can stop or change the character of all the secretions, it can arrest or improve the general nutrition of the body. Every organ and every vital process is represented in the structure of the brain by special centres and groups of cells that have a direct relation with such organs and processes, and through which they are controlled."

One of the greatest of analytical chemists, Baron Justus von Liebig (1803-1873), stated: "Every conception, every mental affection, is followed by changes in the chemical nature of the secreted fluids; and every thought, every sensation, is accompanied by a change in the composition of the substance of the brain." Since Liebig made that assertion, close and thorough investigations have been conducted by Prof. Elmer Gates, the results of which are thus summed up by himself: "My experiments show that irascible, malevolent and depressing emotions generate in the system injurious compounds, some of which are extremely poisonous; also that agreeable, happy emotions generate chemical compounds of nutritive value, which stimulate the cells to manufacture energy."

Mental influence as regards bodily functions is mainly connected with secretions; sometimes they are excited, sometimes checked, and sometimes modified. The sight of food normally causes a flow of saliva. Anger changes the properties of saliva in such a way that they may contain a poison dangerous to life. Fear parches the mouth, a circumstance which gave rise to the Indian custom of aiming at the discovery of a dishonest servant by compelling all the parties likely to have been concerned to hold rice in the mouth for a few minutes. The offender was generally discovered by comparative dryness of the mouthful at the conclusion. Moderate excitement of emotion—whether of grief, of tenderness, or of joy—is often accompanied by a flow of tears. On the other hand, intense grief checks the lachrymal secretion. It is commonly supposed that shedding tears dissipates grief, but, in reality, the tears come because the grief is moderated. Secretions of the breast, just as of the generative organs, are closely connected with emotion and expectation. Impotency in either direction can (and commonly does) occur from mental causes. Strong emotion in a nursing mother has been known to poison her milk so much as to lead to the death of her infant. Sir Samuel Baker remarked that in certain parts of Africa severe grief or anger is almost invariably succeeded by fever.

Bad news is commonly followed by fetid breath, a consequence of morbific matter being excreted through the lungs. Similarly, noxious matter and gas are thrown out in the intestines, and the diarrhœa that is prone to follow certain emotions is partly due to the altered character of the fæces.

A house surgeon of Dr. Durand gave sugared water to a hundred patients, and then announced that it was an emetic given by mistake. Eighty of the hundred patients were violently sick in consequence.

In jaundice, diabetes, hæmorrhage from the lungs, and in a number of other diseased conditions, anger or fear is frequently the main cause.

The effects of mental causes, especially of depressing passions, often pave the way to pulmonary consumption. Not infrequently, after the loss by a family of one member who suffered from that disease, the other members become victims through grief and despondency.

Sir George Paget declared : " In many cases I have seen reason for believing that cancer has had its origin in prolonged anxiety." Dr. Murchison wrote : " I have been surprised how often patients with primary cancer of the liver have traced the cause of this ill-health to protracted grief or anxiety. The cases have been far too numerous to be accounted for as mere coincidences."

Professor Waller mechanically demonstrated that even a passing emotion causes definite changes in the nerve currents in the skin—pleasant thoughts have a bracing effect, unpleasant thoughts a relaxing. More pronounced emotions noticeably affect the efflux of arterial blood to the surface. Mental excitants are liable to induce eczema and other skin diseases, and even dropsy beneath the skin. There is a wide difference in the chemical composition of ordinary perspiration and the sudden, cold exudation which accompanies a deep sense of guilt. The latter kind when brought into contact with selenic acid, produces a characteristically pink hue.

One of Haydn's songs refers to a maiden who " never told her love," but " let concealment, like a worm in the bud, feed on her damask cheek." Why that effect? Every emotion is attended with changes in the cortex, or convolutions of the brain, and these changes generate a force which must be expended in some way. It may take channels which lead to increase of grace and dignity, and the joy of living. If indulged too freely, passion may hold an undesired sway over the reasoning faculties. If, on the other hand, the emotions be unduly suppressed, the energy generated expends itself in hurtful channels. Active exercise may "work off" some of the energy, and also divert attention from a trouble; but *strained* attempts to keep an emotion under, not only cause harm in themselves, they never do more than alter the direction in which the generated force operates. In that way nerve centres are often deranged, and serious nerve, or even lung, disease may result. I shall have more to say on this matter later.

I suppose that the custom of tying a little cotton round a finger, in order to insure recollection of something likely to be forgotten, is known to most of my readers. The same expedient is resorted to in certain parts of Switzerland by females who desire, perhaps on account of some festivity, to delay the menses for a few days. It is said to be usually successful. Certainly mental causes play a large part as regards the menstrual function.

We all know the proverb: "It is worry, not work, that kills." Worry wastes energy and thus tends towards mental and physical inefficiency. It makes the breathing quick and superficial, thus unfavourably affecting the amount of oxygen inhaled and of carbon dioxide exhaled. It interferes with the manufacture of digestive juices, and thus leads to dyspepsia. It unfavourably affects the organs of excretion, not infrequently causing diarrhœa. It alters the chemical composition of the blood and lymph. The combined bad effects inevitably and injuriously load the system with waste products, thus providing a suitable ground for many serious diseases.

Intense mental anguish sometimes leads to insanity.

Before leaving this phase of my subject, I should refer to the so-called ductless glands, the hormones, or "internal secretions," of which are passed into the blood direct. The hormones have properties closely resembling those of drugs. They not only cause some of what are called "symptoms" of emotion, but themselves are very susceptible to emotional influences. The hormones, borne along in the blood-stream, play upon the brain; thus they tend to sustain emotion, favourable or the reverse. When there is a disharmony among the glandular activities, tranquillity does not exist; and with a bad mental outlook, harmony is prevented.

That great Scottish surgeon and teacher of anatomy, John Hunter (1728-1793), asserted : "As one state of the mind is capable of producing a disease, another state of the mind effects a cure." Of course, he did not mean to infer that a disease cannot become intractable, but that, just as one straightens a bent sheet of music by bending it "the other way," so, to cure a complaint, one must reverse the processes that caused it. To that rule I would add that, in order to secure the best possible results, one should aim at bringing the weak parts to an equality with the strong, a chain being "as strong only as its weakest link."

Hope is as beneficial physically as worry is harmful. The action of the heart is improved by hope, respiration becomes fuller, and the various organs of secretion and excretion are favourably affected. Mirth has a health-giving tendency.

Expectation of this or that physical or mental benefit is, as one might suppose, more directly favourable for its realisation than is mere hope. But, of course, the expectation is emotionally tinged. Suppose that a person believes that anger is beneficial physically, although it is not. After the anger is over, if the person expects to derive benefit through the anger itself, he will be happy in the anticipation of the benefit, which state of mind will conduce towards health—although the anger itself could not, unless torpidity of the system was an underlying trouble.

The idea fixed in a sufferer's mind that cure cannot take place can cause any complaint to become chronic, or to progress to a fatal conclusion. Have you ever known any person suffering from pulmonary consumption, and convinced that it is incurable, recover? Nevertheless, post-mortem examinations conducted by Sir (then Professor) William T. Gairdner, late of Glasgow University, showed that 60 per cent. of persons who died from diseases in no way allied to consumption had nevertheless had and recovered from it, as was irrefutably demonstrated by scars on the lungs. The fact is that throughout pulmonary consumption suggestion always plays a big part—albeit seldom recognised. This was clearly evidenced by investigations and experimentation by Louis Rénon, who published details in *Le Monde Medicale* for January 15th, 1914.

The statement is sometimes made that methodical

suggestion cannot cure organic disease, but only functional. These critics assume that a definite division can be made between functional and organic complaints; but it cannot. Further, take the case of ordinary warts. They are decidedly organic, yet Swiss girls of the canton of Vaud, using purely fanciful prescriptions, both cause and remove warts. These phenomena can be caused by hypnotism. The elder Pliny (in his *Natural History*) prescribed as a cure for corns the following : After observing a flight of a meteor, pour a little vinegar on the hinge of a door. If no more, it was well-calculated to corrode the metal!

In his work on *The Breasts* that famous surgeon, Dr. Duncan C. L. Fitzwilliams, asserts : " It is useless to scoff at psychology and mental effect, and to pretend that it has no bearing upon organic disease; it has a decided and beneficial result, even in carcinoma."

The ancient Egyptians used to make amulets from lodestones, and claimed that by contact therewith gouty affections and the toothaches of nervously hysterical persons were cured. In ancient Greece the priests of Æsculapius employed therapetuic methods which in many respects were strange, but which revealed that their employers had a profound recognition of the influence of imagination on health. Priests, concealed in the hollow statues of gods, used to talk to the populace and give them directions or advice as to medicaments and hygiene.

It has been somewhat the same in effect throughout the ages. Nowadays every medical practitioner recognises that indirect suggestion plays a part in the cures attributed to him of adults. "Imagination," declared Sir James Crichton-Browne, "is one of the most effective psychical remedies we have by which we may modify the conditions of health and disease."

The following prescription made the reputation of a young Parisian doctor who ordered it for a lady of Napoleon III's Court .

Aqua sequana	100 gr.
Illa repetita	20 gr.
Eadem	5 gr.

A remarkable cure was effected! Sir William Gull was wont to successfully "gull" his patients with pills made of bread-crumbs and burnt sugar. Sir Andrew Clarke, a physician of Queen Victoria, asserted that when people were ill, what they wanted was something that tasted nasty and would produce an obvious effect; so he usually prescribed sodium bicarbonate, with gentian or bitter aloes—and the desired objects were attained! Many doctors give coloured water to the majority of their patients—"a remedy" which I heard called by Dr. Forbes Winslow, who prescribed it extensively, "Winslow's soothing syrup." Some physicians commonly prescribe "A.D.T."—*i.e.*, "any damned thing." Alongside that prescription may perhaps well be placed the way in which a doctor with whom I was acquainted filled in a certificate to the effect that a certain man was ill and unable to attend work. "What is the nature of the complaint?" was a question the doctor had to answer. That made him scratch his head; but, after a little thought, he confidently wrote "G.O.K.," for he said to himself "God only knows."

Dr. Sutton paradoxically remarked : " If a man is ill enough to say that he is ill when he is not ill, he must be very ill indeed." Why? Because, truly speaking, there is no such thing as an imaginary complaint, although there are complaints of the imagination. But there's the rub! The vast majority of persons have no inkling of the extent to which their own imagination is responsible for their good or bad health. Except with infants and " the lower animals," the unadulterated effect of supposed curative or harmful agents is hardly discoverable. At the back of the patient's mind there is almost always the idea: " This that I am taking," or "doing," or "submitting to has," or "is likely to have," or "may have," "such-and-such an effect." I value hygienic measures, but a prescribed diet, physical culture, or other agent, however well chosen it may happen to be, necessarily owes to imagination part of the value ascribed to itself. It often occurs that the regimen advocated is of little, if any, more value than a bread-and-sugar pill. Conversely, an unfavourable mental attitude may render what would otherwise be useful remedies of little, perhaps no, avail.

Fortunately, it is not necessary to be duped in order to obtain the benefits that imagination can give; and the most powerful remedy is hypnotism. It is true that hysterical paralysis has been removed by an earthquake, but why wait for that agent? Surely, hypnotism is not only equally efficacious, but more easily applied.

CHAPTER IX

PREPARATORY EXPERIMENTS

THE words, "hypnotism" and "suggestion," are often used interchangeably, but their distinction is important. Doubtless, hypnotic *adaptability* exists, and the rôle played by an expert hypnotist resembles in a measure that of an orator, a singer, a writer, an artist, or a sculptor. Frederick the Great always kept a bust of Julius Cæsar on his bureau, for he said that it inspired him to do great things. If, therefore, one uses the words "hypnotism" and "suggestion," interchangeably, a difficulty arises as to what *is not* rather than as to what *is* hypnotism. Considerable confusion would be saved were the word "hypnotism" restricted to its scientific signification—though, as I shall show, there are procedures that merely *lead up to* hypnosis, but are often confused with it, and to which the terms "Donatism" (after Robert Donato) and "Fascination" are particularly applied. The hand-clasping and certain other experiments employed, and given another explanation by Coué, belong to this category. However, it is provable, by observance of physical equivalents of mental states, that he failed to discover their full significance. Some of my readers will doubtless recollect how Coué would insist that persons with whom be employed the hand-clasping experiment, which I shall describe later in this chapter, should clasp their hands together very tightly—" till they tremble," he would say. What was the use of that? Simply this: the muscular cramping detracted from mobility of thought, and a condition opposite to (but useful in the induction of) hypnosis was induced. Why useful in that respect? Because it intensifies the effect of verbal suggestion and also leads to fatigue of attention, which fatigue, in turn, can lead to an entire abandonment of strain, mental as well as physical—exactly what is required as a preparation for the contemplative mood, hypnosis.

To prevent what would be a serious misapprehension, I should say at once that, as persons may operate successfully on one another, the hypnotist need have no more force of character than the hypnotee. Sometimes the operator, and sometimes the subject, does the larger part of the work. Much depends upon the character, training, and preparatory impressions of the subject, and the personality and authority of the operator. While some writers fail to do justice to the part played by the subject, it is just as patent that other writers fail to do justice to the part played by the operator. Of that matter, more anon.

Before dealing with the actual induction of hypnosis, I propose to describe a few experiments (from those I sometimes use in public demonstrations), whereby the induction of hypnosis may be facilitated.

EXPERIMENT 1.—I ask the person to stand with his or her back towards me, and with the eyes closed. I then say: " I want you to picture yourself as on a boat in a harbour, and the boat as moving from right to left—from right to left. The boat is now starting—it is veering round," and so on. It is impracticable to stand motionless for long; but by the suggestions I have given the movements are much beyond what they would otherwise be, and are made in accordance with the imagined movements of the boat. Some subjects stagger, and occasionally someone has symptoms of apparently approaching mal-de-mer. I say " Now, open your eyes, please. You see how imagination can affect your movements.

EXPERIMENT 2.—I take an object (usually a popgun that I use for other illustrative purposes) and, suspending it over the side of the table, I say to the subject, " I want you to look upon your arms as resembling this object—not in appearance, but in that it is hanging limply by means of the string. You see, if I put my hand underneath the object and raise it, I feel its weight; and, if I take my hand away, the object falls. It never remains horizontal after I have taken my hand away. I repeat, then, I want you to look upon your arms as resembling that object—have them quite limp. Have you decided that? "

Should the subject answer in the affirmative, I say, " Very good," and I lift one of his or her arms. In the majority of instances, a person undergoing this experiment for the first time helps to make the movement which he or she expects I am going to perform with his or her arm. In that case I feel the weight has decreased or disappeared, whereas the arm should be lifted as if inanimate.

Even should the arm be dropped relaxed, a few unexpected alternations of arm lifting are nearly always sufficient to lead the subject to expect from my gestures that I am about to lift one or other arm, in which case raising the arm by the subject himself, or herself, is likely to follow. I ask the subject carefully to mark: " It is one thing to *decide upon* relaxation, and another thing to *perform* it "; and I point out that, in effect, *assumption precedes every voluntary action.* Having made my point clear, I continue the experiment until the subject learns to assume readily that upon which he or she has decided.

EXPERIMENT 3.—I ask the subject to stand with his or her back towards me and to close his or her eyes. Then I say, "I am going to ask you, in a moment, to think 'I am falling backward.' You must think intently of falling backward, not reflect as to whether you are going to fall or not, nor think that if you fall you may hurt yourself, nor fall back purposely to please me; but, if you really seem to feel something impelling you to fall backward, you must not resist, but must obey the impulse. I will catch you so that you will not be hurt through falling completely. Now raise your head and close your eyes, please."

I stand a little behind the subject, the left leg forward and the right leg well behind him or her; but towards the close of my experiment I quickly draw back the left leg to prevent the subject hitting the ground. I then lightly rest the tips of the fingers just above the ears of the subject, and say: " Think, I am falling backward." Without pulling the subject in any way, I carry my hands backward, saying meanwhile: " You are falling backward." In some instances the subject makes a slight movement backward, then prevents himself or herself from falling, but usually a complete fall would occur were I not to prevent it. Should the experiment not be completely satisfactory, I inform the subject that he or she has resisted and did not think just of falling, but that falling might cause injury—which accusation is quite true, for otherwise the subject would have fallen like a log.

Before repeating the experiment, I emphasise the fact that the subject must not attempt to *analyse* sensations.

Sometimes I employ falling-forward tests, but with the subject's eyes open. Further explanation on that point is hardly necessary.

EXPERIMENT 4.—I say to the subject: " You know the sensation ' I want to swallow this pill, but I can't? ' The state of mind in such an instance is *in*voluntary. I am going to show you how to get practically the same result voluntarily. I am going to get first the idea of the hands being fixed together.

" Now please to extend your arms in front, the elbows unbent and rigid, and the hands tightly clasped. Think now, ' My hands are glued together, I can't take them apart; I try, but I cannot succeed.' "

The subject who has observed instructions will then make ineffectual efforts to separate his hands, but the greater the effort the tighter the fingers become clasped. In a few moments I say to the subject: " Now think ' I can separate my hands,' " and usually the desired result occurs. Sometimes, however, the idea of disability takes such a hold on the subject's mind that desperate and ineffectual struggling takes place for some little time, in which case I firmly take hold of the clasped hands, and say, calmly but emphatically: "Now stop pulling; I am going to count three, and when I say 'three' your hands will come apart. One, two, three, all right." The hands then separate immediately.

This experiment is admirable for emphasising the fact that the secret of control over one's organism is easy assumption, and that the harder one tries to bring about a phenomenon whilst under the conviction of inability, the more pronounced is the failure.

EXPERIMENT 5.—In order to drive home recognition of the fact that sensations are under the control of thought, I act in this way: I ask a person to close his or her eyes, and then, crossing two of the fingers on one hand of the subject, I move a round object between them. "Can you feel these things moving about?" I ask. "Yes," the person will reply. "How many?" I ask, and usually the answer is "Two." I then say, "Open your eyes and see for yourself how wrong may be your conclusions regarding bodily sensation."

"Now," I add, "please to place one of your hands on my left hand." That done, I slightly extend my right hand, all clenched except the forefinger, in front of the subject's face. I then say very emphatically: "I want you to look upon this forefinger as hot, *very* hot. It is clear that (normally) if a very hot thing touched your hand it would give you a *burning sensation*. Now, sensations are thoughts, and, inasmuch as you are looking upon this finger as hot, when it touches your hand it will give you a burning sensation." I then bring the forefinger gradually downwards and touch the subject's hand, and not infrequently the sensation produced is so marked that the hand may be drawn rapidly away, and the person may even make a kicking movement.

I then say: "Now look upon this finger as most soothing, as if covered with oil!" and I gently rub the place on the hand where the burning was experienced, and, the preceding phenomenon having been experienced, the suggestion of a soothing sensation is actualised at once. I then ask the subject to imagine my forefinger as very, *very* cold—frozen—and thus I lead, by a few little touches, to corresponding sensations of cold.

EXPERIMENT 6.—I ask the subject to feel his or her pulse. Then I say: "I want to show you how easy it is to vary the pulse rate. Count the throbs. Now think: 'Quicker, quicker, quicker!'" (I speak this in a lively way); then, after a pause, I say: "Slower, slower" (calmly and emphatically). "Think now: 'My pulse will miss one throb!'"

All these experiences can be readily obtained by leading the subject calmly to assume, and, by this means, he or she becomes ready for the development of definite hypnosis.

CHAPTER X

THE INDUCTION AND TERMINATION OF HYPNOSIS

I SHALL here deal with procedures which especially apply to hypnotism when the operator and subject are together, and shall deal in a later chapter with radio-hypnotism, and so on.

The method of induction I shall first describe combines the main procedure of Braid with that of the Nancy School.

The subject is seated, or reclines, comfortably, with his back towards the source of light. An object is then held about a foot from and slightly above his eyes, and he is asked to gaze steadily at that object. By compliance with this direction fatigue is gradually induced and the subject is led to strain in order to continue to stare steadily. (In straining he *cramps* his *attention.*) At first the pupils of his eyes are slightly contracted, owing to the situation of the object; but the strain leads to relaxation of the optic muscles, and the pupils then dilate—a sign of dimness of vision. The greater the effort to attend, the quicker is the respiration. Tact is required here in order to decide as to the advisability or otherwise of employing *verbal suggestion* to bring, or hasten, the desired results. When physical symptoms denote that directly the subject experiences strain he figuratively draws back, verbal suggestion is advisable. Many operators fail to exercise adequate discrimination here, and, by employing suggestion unnecessarily and imprudently, not infrequently hinder, or even prevent, the desired end.

As a general rule, suggestions should begin by stating what *has* occurred, and should gradually lead up to what has not occurred, but what it is intended *shall* occur. Thus the operator may say: " Your eyelids feel heavy, your eyes tired. You feel sleepy. Your arms feel heavy. Your legs feel heavy. You can scarcely keep your eyes open. They are closing, and you are letting go all effort. You are resting placidly. You attend to nothing but my voice." Some operators suggest: " You are fast asleep." Unless the subject understands that in this connection the word " sleep " signifies " placidity," it should not be employed, both because of the misapprehension and because its employment risks the causing of spurious phenomena.

Nevertheless, there are very pronounced symptoms of genuine hypnotisation, and the expert operator watches for their appearance. At the moment when all effort is abandoned, there is a deep sigh—as of relief—and closure of the eyelids, which, however, may tremble for a few moments. During the induction, breathing is slightly quickened, but, following the involuntary sigh to which I have referred, it becomes slower and deeper than usual.

Quickening of respiration inevitably occurs when there is continuous strain—consequently tissue waste—whether muscular or mental in character. Passions and emotions which excite the brain have a similar effect, and thus tend to debilitate; whereas placidity of thought and feeling are accompanied by comparatively slow and steady respiration, and thus tend towards longevity. Profound thinkers commonly breathe deeply and steadily. Observation of respiration, and consequent deductions therefrom, were of service to me in confirming my theory of hypnotism, and to all they can prove valuable as important checks on the subject's mental conditions.

Whilst all the physical stimuli employed tend eventually to bring about a similar result, some do it by so increasing nervous irritability that a sudden suspension of all strain takes place, whereas others are of a soothing character.

The old " magnetists " relied mainly upon soothing processes. The physical part of their treatment was mostly administered by the hands, and was therefore termed " manipulation." The movements of the hands they called " passes." Passes may be either *with* contact (*strong* or *light*) or *without*. If without, and of any *physical* utility, they are performed near enough to the subject to make a sensible effect upon his or her skin. To ensure that effect, in making the passes the fingers should be bent so as to make a kind of scoop of the hands. Between each pass (*i.e.*, whilst the hands are returning to the position for another pass to commence) the fingers should be separated, and the hands flattened, and moved some distance from the body of the subject. To induce the so-called "trance" the passes are made *downward*, often from the head to the knees of the subject, whilst, to dissipate the trance, the effective passes are made *upward*. The magnetists laid great stress upon the direction of the passes, and they were right. I tested the effects respectively of downward and upward passes upon each of my children when babes of a few days; downward passes led to sleep, whereas upward passes awakened. In adults there apparently is a tendency to cerebral anæmia or cerebral congestion respectively, in accordance with the direction of attention.

Mesmerists often requested subjects to look into their (the operators') eyes, but such fixed gaze was usually not continued so long as to cause definite fatigue, the subjects being told to close their eyes as soon as the inclination occurred.

In passing, I should remark that I consider in error those who imagine that the use of the eyes by a hypnotist is practically identical with that of other bright objects. Facial expression can do much towards inspiring confidence, and may be made to suggest the appearance of certain phenomena. In numerous cases I have succeeded, by changing my facial expression "in accordance with the specific indications of the case" in inducing within a few moments a deep hypnosis.

Specific verbal suggestion was but little employed by mesmerists, consequently the tendency to spurious phenomena, except such as were the result of the subject's design, were avoided in a measure.

The results of mesmeric processes are usually brought about only gradually. The earliest sign of success is a tendency to bodily repose, a disinclination to move. The eyelids droop, and the temperature of the extremities falls. Eventually the eyes usually close, the expression of the face becomes very placid, and respiration slow and deep. The person appears to be asleep, but when addressed, arouses—without, however, losing the placid expression of the features.

Some mesmerists have maintained that hypnotism is but a coarse form of mesmerism—that penetration and clear-headedness are marked and distinct features of persons in the mesmeric condition. There seems to be an element of truth in the distinction. Compared with the drastic method of Braid, for example, the mesmeric processes are more economic of nerve energy. Preliminary strain, being somewhat like a narcotic, lessens the subject's available power of actualising suggestion. Further, if the subject be of a very suggestible nature and the operator unskilful, a subject may be spoiled, through drastic measures, for future occasions. Failure on the part of operators to recognize spurious phenomena is apt to mislead subjects strangely. The skilful operator so acts that the condition induced can be deepened and developed.

One advantage, however, attaches to drastic measures; they save time. This often means a saving of expense, and, as a second "hypnotisation" is usually easy, a stringent method is sometimes advisable in the first place—with certain plethoric persons especially.

It is with procedures as with drugs; much depends upon idiosyncrasies—upon constitution and attitude.

The task of the operator is to find and apply the most suitable procedures for each case. In so doing, caution is requisite. Fatiguing the sense of sight is not devoid of danger—instead the operator may direct his subject to listen to the ticking of a clock. A method valuable in certain cases is to direct the subject to contract the chest and then breathe as little as possible, whereby a drowsiness is inducible, as when one comes out of the fresh air into a close room. The Fakirs of India are credited with inducing long trances (not hypnoses) by thrusting the tip of the tongue between the posterior nares and the oral cavity, thus partially suspending animation. In the West Indies, slaves were known to bring about their own death purposely by the referred-to interference with respiration.

The operator may sometimes find advisable the taking of bromide of potassium (or even the inhalation of chloroform) by the subject.

The most serviceable methods of inducing hypnosis are usually such as strike the happy medium.

Dr. Sidney Flower's method is one worthy of especial mention, for it is easy, not sensational, gets the necessary attention, and yet is sufficiently monotonous to induce an inclination to slumber. This method consists of a combination of counting, shutting and opening the eyes, and verbal suggestion. The operator counts slowly, and the subject is required to open his eyes for a moment at each number. The subject usually becomes sleepy very soon; his eyelids open with difficulty, and then remain closed—the eyebrows perhaps being raised from time to time, instead of the eyelids being separated. A few reassuring suggestions alone are usually required.

In accordance with the observable peculiarities regarding respiration, leisurely deep breathing is useful as a hypnotic artifice, and in that connection, as will be described later, I have long employed it.

The statement has often been made that hypnosis is obviously identical with sleep, inasmuch as such communication can be established with sleeping persons that hypnotic phenomena are inducible in them. Personal experimentation convinced me that, in reality, the person thus operated upon is partially awakened. The first attempt to effect the transition may result, unless very gentle, in a complete awakening. As a special precaution, it is usual to give the subject a preparatory intimation. The communication between the sleeper and the operator is best begun otherwise than verbally; passes without contact, or very gentle stroking of the forehead may be employed. After thus performing for a minute or so, the operator may commence the giving of gently-whispered suggestions, somewhat as follows: " You will not arouse. You are quite placid," and so on. (Short sentences are preferable to long.) When some sign of recognition has been obtained from the subject, the operator may gradually lead up to the ordinary speaking tone, and " develop " the hypnosis.

The training in some cases can be rapid, in others needs repeated operations. A transition can be very rapidly brought about with persons who have previously been hypnotised.

Dr. Mesnet, writing in 1894, asserted that he had effected hypnosis through giving suggestions at the moment of a person's awaking from spontaneous somnambulism. The reader will perceive that Mesnet's contention in no way conflicts with my own.

Inasmuch as placidity is the basis of hypnosis, wonder should not be excited by the fact that with some persons a primary hypnosis can be induced almost immediately and even whilst they remain standing. The ordinary process in such cases is for the subject to face the operator whilst suggestions of sleep, drowsiness, or placidity are given. (Were the change in respiration observed in such instances, the prevalent confusion of hypnotism with Donatism would not exist.)

After the subject has thoroughly learned his part, not even the process referred to is needed, hypnosis being inducible at a mere signal from the operator, consequently in response to the subject's own suggestion. Closing of the eyes by the subject is not essential, though helpful.

Auto-hypnosis is the trick of so-called exposers of hypnotism, who, according to their own accounts, have voluntarily deceived the public for years, and then suddenly have turned so good as to resolve to tell the public all they know for—the highest fees they can obtain.

Perhaps I ought to mention that Dr. Alexander Cannon has described what he has called the " Bernheim-Coué method " of inducing hypnosis. As the collaborator and authorised biographer of Coué, I am entitled to emphasise that the measures thus described are, in certain respects, directly contrary to what Coué advocated, and include coloured lights and the employments of Cannon's own gramophone records! Coué published a wholesale condemnation of the introduction of colour-schemes in connection with his method.

It is a common and harmful error to suppose that hypnosis *in itself* presents any difficulty as regards termination. The difficulty lies not in dissipating, but in perpetuating, hypnosis—a truth as evident from experience as from recognition of the actual nature of the condition. Ways of terminating hypnosis are either what are in reality mere signals to the subject, or processes calculated to dissipate any drowsiness that may be present. A drastic method of hypnotising, and also expectancy, sometimes causes extreme drowsiness, or even a slumber slightly resembling the coma of drunkenness. In such an instance it is advisable to refrain from arousing the subject; he will probably pass into a profound sleep and awaken much refreshed. Should circumstances necessitate awakening, blowing on the face, or tapping on the soles of the feet, generally suffices.

There are a *few* cases in which imagination proceeding from ignorance leads to some little difficulty in dissipating drowsiness. This, I repeat, is not dangerous, though it may sometimes cause inconvenience; consequently, operators ought, in questionable cases, to give a preparatory suggestion during the induction of hypnosis.

CHAPTER XI

THE MANAGEMENT OF HYPNOSIS

It is most important to observe that preliminary notions (perhaps entirely wrong) of a person relative to hypnosis and the after-effects of treatment may be actualised when that person is hypnotised. In that case there is pre-hypnotic suggestion. When the continuance in " normal " life of some phenomenon induced during hypnosis is desired, or when some other change is desired to occur after hypnosis, the operator can (and ordinarily should) make *verbal* suggestions to that effect. Such suggestions are post-hypnotic. Formerly much error accumulated through the non-recognition of the part played by *pre*-hypnotic suggestion, and much work was spoiled by non-recognition of the uses of *post*-hypnotic suggestion.

It was said of Edmund Gurney, the hypnotic investigator that he never succeeded in getting a first hypnosis in anyone, consequently had to use for his experiments persons previously hypnotised by someone else. That relation is clearly explicable on the ground of confusion regarding the actual nature of hypnosis (he obviously was confused in trying to distinguish between genuine and spurious phenomena), and therefore does not show that the most difficult part of the operator's work is necessarily, as is generally supposed, the induction of hypnosis. Far more skill is requisite to utilise the condition skilfully than to induce it.

An eminent Swedish brain specialist, Oedmann by name, admitted that though he himself could not cure dipsomaniacs by hypnotism, when he sent them to Dr. Wetterstrand, of Stockholm, a cure invariably occurred. Expectation is frequently at work where little expected: it is concerned with so-called "divining" by rods as to the whereabouts of water or metal (a blindfolded "diviner" is a failure) and a host of other phenomena. Apparently, expectation entered largely into Mesmer's success, and doubtless into Wetterstrand's. But what had Wetterstrand himself to tell us? "The patients cannot, and should not, be treated in the same way, and, therefore, the physician's psychological experience has here a very wide range. Some are to be approached sternly, others mildly, this one must be reasoned with, and that one, more susceptible, submits, perhaps, to the therapeutic suggestion." It is evident, therefore, that skill, rather than the subject's expectation, accounted for Wetterstrand's success; and, so far as I personally am concerned, of the cures I have been instrumental in bringing about, many were of persons who, though they yielded to the solicitations of their friends or relations to come for treatment, up to the time of actual treatment were utterly unconvinced as to the possibility of obtaining any benefit therefrom.

However, very much depends upon the personality of the operator. Putting aside mere hypnotic entertainers, a good hypnotist (in the higher sense) must have a sympathetic nature, but it should not be too mellow. The wish to do good is far from enough. He should have *suavitèr in modo*, but *fortitèr in re*—should be gentle in manner, but vigorous in deed. He should aim, too, at so thoroughly realising his client's point of view that there will spring up between the two a very real sympathy. The client should become convinced that the operator has not only sympathy, but the knowledge and skill required to help him or her. A passive sympathy is an incomplete one; if the sympathy be complete, it infallibly leads to action.

It does not follow invariably that the hypnotist should explain to persons the full rationale of treatment; indeed, there are persons so unintelligent that to attempt any such explanation would pave the way to failure, for they cannot be made to understand the force resident within themselves. Nevertheless, I believe in being quite frank whenever so doing is not liable to prove injurious to the client. One noted hypnotist, Dr. Moll, declared that if a patient believed in the efficacy of a pilgrimage to a shrine, he (Moll) would consider it his duty to recommend it.

Where confidence as regards either integrity or skill in the hypnotist is lacking, failure is likely to occur. Distrust of the operator interferes with the induction, by distracting the subject's attention, thus depriving him (temporarily) of part of his powers of responsiveness, and by inclining to affect the hypnotist unfavourably. Obviously, the value to the hypnotist of a reputed attribute of absolute integrity can hardly be over estimated. I venture to add that, although " hallucinations " and " illusions " of the very suggestible may amuse spectators, such experimentation is hardly likely to lead the subject to feel kindly towards the operator. Distrust of integrity or of ability is very liable to arise instead.

Personal influence depending upon individuality, it can happen that a subject is partially, or even entirely, impervious to the attempts of an expert hypnotist, and yet may succumb to an inferior operator.

Much of the poor work accomplished by hypnotists is due to their not having thoroughly (perhaps not at all) grasped the importance of taking a particular section of their clients back to what may be described as " the fork in the road," and thereby giving them a new orientation. More is said on this matter in chapters 8, 14 and 19.

Further, many operators do not seem adequately to realise the meaning of the word " suggestion." An operator cannot obtain anything approaching uniformly good results unless he realise that he ought to convey to the subject far more than mere words; one needs to convey ideas—ay, and states of feeling. Language, indeed, comprises any and every means by which what passes in one mind may be made known to another. An individual commonly employs various forms of language simultaneously, but it often occurs that the language of nature—of tones, looks and gestures, of *emotions*—gives the lie to the words uttered. A duty of the hypnotist lies in conveying to, and impressing upon, his subjects the *right* ideas; but, where minds are not tuned akin, the difficulty attendant upon that aim is more than a novice is likely to suppose. The same word or phrase conveys widely different meanings to different people. Words are far from being a perfect vehicle for the transmission of ideas—a fact forcefully illustrated by the disputes so common on abstract matters. The hypnotist needs to use the right words for each case, and not only "the sound" of his voice, but *his whole manner*, should be "an echo to the sense"; then the signification of the words is enhanced, not disguised. Well says an Arabian proverb: "He is the best orator who can turn men's ears into eyes."

The hypnotic operator should not be looked upon, nor look upon himself, in the light of a master who gives orders, but rather as a friend, a guide, who leads his client step by step along the road to health and happiness. Nevertheless, the expert suggestionist not only *directs* the attention of whomever he treats, he inspires him, he holds up before him mental pictures which (unless the subject be purposely inattentive, which can happen) assist in imparting a something whereby the requisite assumptions can come about. A good hypnotist has enthusiasm for his work, or dramatic ability, and the best hypnotists have both.

Space precludes my entering into particulars regarding elocution, but, for the sake of persons desirous of becoming competent hypnotists, I should like to give a few hints. Attempts to teach elocution by means of a study of inflections and such like are always fallacious, and for the simple reason that the inflections present in ordinary speech reveal the attitude of the speaker's mind. The force of what one says depends largely upon the mental condition immediately preceding and accompanying speech. The painter has a mental picture first, does not put his brush to the canvas before deciding upon the stroke that he should make. Similarly, the speaker should never be in a hurry. Pauses, indeed, are as requisite to a speaker as to the person or persons addressed, the mind requiring time to formulate, as well as to receive, an idea. During the pauses the speaker's attention should not drift: his imagination should be at work, and there should be a gathering together of forces, in preparation for what is to follow. Do not hunt for suitable words, or they will evade you. As the idea becomes clearly outlined, becomes definite, corresponding words occur to one. The mood gives rise to the idea, and the idea to the actions of speech—much as vivid imagination of kicking leads, not infrequently, to the corresponding action. Dramatic power is the result of mass of feeling, not of conscious attempt at loudness. Persons not uncommonly speak louder in order to heighten an effect; they are forgetful, or unaware, that soft tone may be very forceful, may show by its intensity that a mass of feeling is being suppressed. Should a required state of mind not come readily, meet it half-way by assuming and yielding to the physiological equivalents. If you turn up the corners of your lips and simultaneously endeavour to think a sad thought, or turn them down and attempt a bright thought, you find yourself defeated.

From the preceding remarks it is apparent that, when the operator employed is skilful, the subject's eyes may advantageously be opened during the treatment. This is very important in certain cases. But, of course, all hypnotic treatment should be carefully adapted to individual requirements. Just as very stupid persons should not have the rationale of hypnotic treatment told to them, so, with very intelligent subjects, ordinary verbal suggestion may often be advantageously dispensed with, and, instead, the persons be requested to think in certain ways—and even where alterations of mental attitude are sought. The placidity of hypnosis is apt to enable subjects to look through favourable glasses, and to see the advisability of assuming a reasonably optimistic attitude. When hypnosis is used solely for suggestive purposes, the lighter the condition the longer the time that should be spent on a treatment. On an average, a quarter of an hour for treatment is advisable; the current of thought has to be altered, and undesirable ideas crowded out by the instilling of new ones. If, on the other hand, post-hypnotic amnesia be induced, less suggestive treatment suffices, unwelcome reflection being less likely to occur.

Patients sometimes substitute one harmful habit for another—a person who has been helped to throw aside smoking may turn to alcoholism. That is because the habit was but a symptom of a hidden craving, which hidden craving requires searching for and dealing with in a manner favourable to the patient's well-being. Often it is advisable to endeavour to divert purposely the patient's energies into a useful channel, often advisable to encourage interest in a new pursuit. Some subjects surpass what the hypnotist suggests.

Whatever a hypnotist does suggest ought to be carefully adapted to the client's case, not only as regards the past and present, but also the future. A suggestion given one day should not need contradicting another day. A lady came to me for the purpose of having eradicated the love she bore for a man who did not return the affection, but with whom she was continually in contact. I asked her whether she had reflected as to the results likely to follow the suggestion she desired me to make. I found her judgment on that point not above criticism, and I told her that if I consented to do as she asked, it would be on condition that if she were not satisfied with the result she would return to me. She consented, and I treated her accordingly; but a few days later she came to see me again and told me that since her first visit she had spent a most unhappy time, that she felt that there was "a something" missing, and would I, she asked, restore the love she had voluntarily relinquished. I did as requested. A week or two passed, then the lady turned up again. "I find," she said, "that this state is nearly as bad as the other, so I want you please to make me neither in love nor indifferent." That seemed to solve the problem!

In any case I prefer that treatments should be repeated once at least. (Some cases demand frequent treatment.) To attempt too much at a treatment is sometimes equivalent to losing nearly all. Moreover, if one is enamoured of one's work, and is also competent, by observing the effect of a single treatment much can be learned that can be turned to the client's advantage in another.

When the inculcation of principles is required, *lethargy* in the subject is desirable; but when training (in hypnosis) of a faculty is required, the *alert* state is necessary.

Hypnotic treatment often proves useful in that by means of it a patient may be helped to adhere to other means indicated as essential to cure. It is true that by suggesting that the lungs will function better, fuller and more regular breathing can usually be procured, but not nearly to the extent that occurs when systematic and well-regulated exercise of the respiratory organs is made a particular study. Through hypnotic suggestion the patient may persevere with even what would otherwise be disregarded. If, as sometimes occurs, training whilst in hypnosis is practicable, it should by all means be resorted to, the mental and physical condition of the patient then being most favourable.

Sometimes an induced phenomenon (*e.g.,* the absence of pain) is retained after hypnosis inasmuch as such retention is assumed by the subject. Often, however, an assurance from the hypnotist is necessary —always advisable

A subject left alone is apt to become abstracted; consequently, to prevent any possible wrong assumptions, it is sometimes advisable to dissipate the hypnosis directly the curative suggestions have been given. In sure instances, delayed dehypnotization benefits by encouraging digestion, assimilation, and utilisation of already accepted suggestions.

CHAPTER XII

MEDICAL AND SURGICAL USES.

THE great physiologist and psychologist, Professor W. B. Carpenter, stated long ago his conviction that hypnotism, " if applied with skill and discrimination," " would take rank as one of the most potent methods of treatment which the physician has at his command." Hypnotism is useful as a healing agent for various reasons, some of which are the following:—

(1) The induction of hypnosis trains the subject in getting a condition of rest, and in that way may help materially as regards the cure of insomnia, nervousness, and so on.

(2) Hypnosis itself is a very restful condition. Long hypnoses have been found very valuable as part of the treatment of pulmonary consumption and other diseases of debility.

(3) Hypnotic suggestion can supplant wrong thought by right thought, so that there can be established favourable functioning of the various parts of the organism.

(4) Hypnosis is a favourable condition for revealing mental causes of physical and mental disability and disease.

When organs or parts are diseased, there is always a deficiency or excess in the supply of nerve energy. Hypnotism can enable, or help to enable, the brain to redistribute nerve energy, can also assist the organs of digestion, of secretion, and excretion, and thus may cure, or assist in curing, many complaints which otherwise would become chronic or might even progress to a fatal conclusion.

But every complaint has a mental factor; and in many cases this mental factor represents as much as 99 per cent. of the whole complaint. It is among such cases that sudden cures occur that are sometimes described as "miraculous." But in most cases of disease an attitude favouring recovery is usually inducible by hypnotic treatment. Cheerfulness and expectation of improvement can usually be assured. Further, the patient may be led to persevere with the needed regimen, so the chances of recovery and renewed vigour are much enhanced. Methodical suggestion can lead to toleration—or even enjoyment—of formerly disliked articles of diet, and thus what is called "psychic" or "appetite" juice is automatically secreted and the digestion favoured. The patient may be enabled to dislike and discard unsuitable articles of diet. Therefore, to reserve hypnotism as a last resource is a grievous error, for (normally) he or she who is not persevering will not persevere in persevering.

The power which hypnotism has of dissipating fears often performs signal service: I have successfully treated cases in which dire effects had proceeded from fear of such diseases as consumption and cancer. Fear itself should be viewed as a disease—a disease which paves the way for more serious evils. It certainly renders persons liable to contagion, during epidemics especially.

The capacity of hypnotism to overcome pain is valuable. Pain, though a protection in some ways, is often a great evil. Take pain from a wound and the healing processes tend to be much hastened thereby—a fact strikingly illustrated by operations rendered partially or completely painless by hypnotism. On the other hand, attention to pain increases its intensity: indeed to imagine a pain is, in a sense, to have one; and an imagined pain tends to lead to recognisable physical damage. Chronic complaints in many instances become so by a cumulative process—physical trouble, fear, and probably worry, combined; and the finish of an actual complaint often is followed by a complaint of the imagination.

Though complaints of a nervous or functional character are those most amenable to cure or benefit by hypnotism solely, there is scarcely any complaint unsuitable for such treatment used alongside other measures. For example: in incipient pulmonary consumption, hypnotic treatment is not to be recommended by itself, but it can lead to better functioning (through the bettered mental state) of the heart, lungs, digestive and excretive organs, and so on. There are also the advantages that it almost assures the patient's compliance with the advisable diet and curative movements, that it conduces to bodily comfort and peace of mind—both favourable adjuncts—and that, incidentally, it teaches and establishes a habit of recuperative relaxation.

Through the agency of hypnotism, physical strength can apparently be enormously increased, as is sometimes exemplified on the stage by " cataleptic " (" stiffening ") feats. The true explanation is that the subject *economises* his nervous and muscular energy—for hypnotism does not add any material to the person's organism. The fact remains (indeed is suggested by the circumstances referred to) that hypnosis is an ideal condition for drill. Used in connection with calisthenics, hypnotism can prove extraordinarily efficacious. In effect, Braid showed this by remarkable cures of spinal curvature. Similarly, by hypnotism combined with deft direction I have cured a considerable number of cases of writers'-cramp and similar affections.

Such culture can extend to the various sense-organs. Certain defects of vision (many of my clients have been enabled to throw aside glasses), blindness due to functional paralysis of the optic nerve, and a host of cases of deafness, and some of loss of smell, are readily curable through hypnotism. I should say in passing that hundreds of times I have demonstrated before public audiences that sight and hearing in most persons are " normally " astonishingly less than what they are in reality. More will be said of this later.

The pretension—made in a book by one practitioner—that he enabled a blind person without a retina (the nervous background of the eye) to see temporarily with the soul is—to put it mildly—fantastic.

Hypnotic suggestion can stimulate or inhibit feeling. I have cured extreme ticklishness.

Anæsthesia (absence of feeling) or analgesia (absence of pain) can often be induced by hypnotism. Indeed, it was in connection with surgery that hypnotism (then called "animal magnetism" or "mesmerism") first came into prominence in this country, but it was supplanted by chloroform, etc.—more convenient and reliable agents. However, where there is heart weakness, only hypnotism is safe, and when any subject has previously been rendered analgesic by that agent, it should by all means be employed in preference to other agents. Limbs and breasts may be amputated, tumours cut away, accouchements may be painless (the contractions have been even arrested, and the confinement delayed for a week), teeth extracted without pain—in short, the sphere of hypnotic analgesia is, with certain persons and under certain conditions, equivalent to that of surgery.

I would here emphasise the fact that hypnotic analgesia does not necessitate the induction of a condition the events of which are forgotten. In the case of my two sons confinement was painless, and only a partial lapse of memory followed. At the birth of the second child I acted as accoucheur.

Certain ecstatics, from extreme emotion when meditating on the wounds of Christ, were so carried beyond normal sensibility, that (it was asserted) they suffered from erythematous circles, weals, or even bleeding. Louise Lateau and Catherine Emmerich were two modern instances closely observed. But such stigmata can be induced experimentally by means of hypnotic suggestion. So may the appearance of a burn. Should those facts excite surprise in view of those mentioned in my eighth chapter?

No wonder that the Church of Rome cautiously declares, regarding the alleged miracles at Lourdes, Loretto, Echternach, and other shrines, that its members may accept them or reject them in accordance with individual estimates of the evidences produced! If a person professes to be divinely commissioned and claims as evidence something he does that can also be done by persons not claiming a divine commission, his claim should go for nothing. On the other hand, a person may be able to perform a reputed miracle through greater knowledge or skill in certain respects than is ordinarily possessed. An unscrupulous business man, conversant with my writings and demonstrations, once got into personal touch with me and proposed that, instead of endeavouring to tell the truth about hypnotism, I should join him in founding a new religion, of which I should be the thaumaturgist, or miracle-worker. He contended, I suspect with truth, that the proposition would be a very paying one, and was disagreeably surprised when I declined to entertain it for a moment. I did not trouble to ascertain particulars of his scheme; I was to be the miracle-worker (that much was clear), and as to him—well, perhaps his part was to be the profit!

The claim that hypnotism can enable persons to partake to any desired extent of alcohol, and yet remain sober, is contrary to fact; but a hysterical tendency to drunken symptoms *can* be combated successfully by hypnotism.

It is impracticable to give in small space anything approaching a complete list of the directions in which hypnotism may be beneficially employed—of course, often in conjunction with other agents. The following list is intended to include the more pronounced:—

Alcoholism, Opsomania (gluttony), Morphinism, Cocainism, Stammering, Stuttering, certain other speech defects, Sexual Perversion, Excessive Nocturnal Emissions, Masturbation, Bed-wetting, Chorea (St. Vitus' Dance), certain cases of Asthma, Neuritis, Neuralgia, Neurasthenia, Psychasthenia, Headache, Earache, Singing in the Ears, certain forms of Rheumatism, Insomnia, Sleep-walking, Uneasy Dreams, Functional Paralysis, Blindness from functional paralysis of the optic nerve, various other eye troubles, Functional Deafness, Functional Loss of Smell, many cases of Loss of Voice, Telegraphists' and Writers' Cramp, Spasmodic Wry Neck, Hypochondria, Hysteria, certain cases of Epilepsy, Bashfulness, Nervousness, Delusions, Dominant Ideas, Incipient Melancholia, certain cases of Heart Trouble, Irregularities of Menstruation, other female complaints, Dyspepsia and Constipation, Loss of Appetite, Defective Circulation, Excessive Perspiration, Shingles, Sea and Railway Sickness, Extreme Ticklishness, Housemaid's Knees, certain Growths, Blushing and various Skin Complaints.

CHAPTER XIII

CO-OPERATIVE TREATMENT.

In my eleventh chapter I referred to the use alongside hypnotism of other aids to health. My book *Hypnotism, the Friend of Man,* dealt in considerable detail with my attitude to medical theories, and I do not propose to enter into details here. A fact which I should emphasise is that when two modes of treatment are employed simultaneously in dealing with a case, each may help the other, or may neutralise it—even completely. I hold that ostensible remedies should be so chosen and combined as to secure a maximum effect, and that physically hygienic measures should in general be united to mental.

Dr. Charles Singer, lecturer on the history of medicine in the University of London, frankly pointed out: "Works on medicine intended for popular consumption are often couched in the jubilant terms of victory. Yet there are whole departments in which no progress whatever has been made." But why? Dr. Robert Bell, who was awarded, in 1912, £2,000 damages against the British Medical Association, in an action which arose out of an article (entitled "Cancer, Credulity, and Quackery") in the *British Medical Journal,* insisted that what is supposed to be medical science is founded on wrong foundations. "No laboratory," he wrote, "will ever be able to find a substitute for hygienic living, or an antidote to an unwholesome diet or a pernicious environment." "It is impossible," he declared, "to inject serum derived from diseased animals into the human blood without seriously and permanently impairing the vital energy of the various cells which compose the body into which it is introduced, for it reduces the resisting power to disease." He condemned vaccination and other forms of inoculation as being "the irrational policy of men who, to put it mildly, were trifling with human life."

Lord Bacon, in his *Advancement of Learning,* stated: "Medicine is a science which hath been more professed than laboured, and yet more laboured than advanced; the labour having been, in my judgment, rather in circle than in progression." Notwithstanding improvements in some directions, results still justify that view.

I have no intention of following the example of the raw recruit who maintained that every soldier except himself was out of step. What I propose to do is to refer to my general attitude to diet and curative movements, and then to cite a few examples of my own procedures in practice.

Though the idea is naïve that the digestive organs are capable of, and accustomed to, picking out the good and rejecting the bad, irrespective of the materials supplied, the fact that the system can and does exercise the power of selecting one harmful substance instead of another for excretion, leaving the less harmful substances to be dealt with later, perhaps temporarily tolerated—inasmuch as work more important to the well-being of the organism is on hand—can be chemically demonstrated. Further: many deadly poisons are but combinations of harmless elements—*e.g.*, hydrocyanic (prussic) acid and the alkaloids are combinations of hydrogen, carbon and nitrogen. Is the fact surprising that a person may eat the purest food and his diet may be balanced to a nicety, and nevertheless his attitude of mind may be so unfavourable that the food is rendered of practically no effect, or may even be turned into poison? And, apparently, the converse is to some extent true: a favourable mental attitude can enable the system to do its best with the materials supplied, though, from the standpoint of chemistry, they may be very far from ideal.

Dietetic, like other, extremists are prone to be nearly as wide of the mark as are those they condemn most heartily.

There is a prevalent notion that unless a person be adopting the dogmas of some special dietetic cult, he or she is not feeding rightly. And yet, the cults disagree widely!

The main complaint is that ordinary diet introduces into one's system waste and injurious materials. In point of fact: whatever one eats, that disadvantage is bound to occur in degree, our food being taken largely from things—vegetable and animal—that have lived primarily for themselves, not for us, and, like us, have had to fend for themselves. An old Roman writer,

Pliny, argued in this way: "Wherefore has our mother the earth brought forth so many deadly drugs, but that, when wearied with suffering, we may employ them for suicide?"

In point of fact, people diet in so many different ways and yet get equally good—or equally bad—results.

Individual experiments in dieting are nearly always misleading. The circumstances preceding, accompanying and following the taking of the various and varying foods, and also the mental factor (a strong one) are likely to be overlooked partially, or even completely. There is the question of idiosyncrasy, too.

Drastic alterations in diet are rarely (though sometimes) essential, and may be impracticable. A few general hints usually suffice.

Among aids to health, particular attention to one may compensate to some extent for neglect of another.

The fact must never be ignored that attention to vital organs is of extreme importance; often a rigid diet is advised when the real need is the strengthening, by movements, of parts of the digestive apparatus. Moreover, an unfavourable mental attitude may be the only serious obstacle.

I have insisted, throughout my professional career, upon the need of comprehensiveness in dealing with disease. Some of the significant results of such treatment will now be detailed by me.

Before me is a letter from a lady—the wife of a business man holding a prominent position. The communication illustrates the fact that the measures I employ have not fundamentally altered, for it was written in July, 1914. The lady wrote that her experiences reminded her of " the woman, mentioned by the evangelist Mark, who ' had suffered many things of many physicians, and had spent all that she had, and was nothing bettered but rather grew worse.' " The letter gave the following particulars: " During a period of seventeen years, I suffered from movable kidneys, nervous dyspepsia, much corpulence, neuritis, gout, defective sight—which was rapidly becoming worse and worse when I consulted you—and a continuous headache. Drugs, electricity, Turkish baths, mustard packs, brine baths (Droitwich), massage, hydro-treatment, rest cure and ' nerve foods ' (Sanatogen, etc.), are only a few of the ' remedies ' tried by me and found ineffectual. I also went about, by advice, from one seaside place to another, but no benefit resulted.

" I consulted," she continued, " nearly thirty ' qualified ' medical men—many of them specialists. I was also treated by physical culture methods by Mr. Eugen Sandow, and by Mr. Eustace Miles (for six months) by physical culture combined with ' uric-acid-free ' diet. I was worse after receiving their treatment than before I commenced. No better results followed a month's hypnotic treatment by Dr. Lloyd Tuckey. His final conclusion was that I must always treat myself as an invalid and lie on my back most of the time. ' I am sorry,' he said, ' but I cannot do anything for you.' That decision almost made me decide to undergo an operation declared by Dr. Suckling and another medical man to be the only remedy. The operation consisted of attaching the kidneys to the ribs." (Only indirectly, of course.) " However, hearing about you, I applied with the hope that you might possibly overcome an intense nervousness which made me quite unable to go out by myself. But I never for a moment imagined that you would be able to restore my health, and was greatly astonished when you said that that was possible. However, from the very commencement, I was greatly benefited, my eyes have been considerably rejuvenated, and with some persistence I have become strong and well—indeed, better than I ever remember to have been. I never have even an occasional headache now. Such diet, curative movements and hypnotism as you employ are doubtless capable of performing wonders, and I hold you are completely justified in describing them as 'a *complete* rational treatment of disease.' To have known you earlier would have meant to me the saving of hundreds of pounds."

The writer of that letter proved an ardent supporter of my methods, and gave me the opportunity, if I so decided, to make public use of her name. I refrained from doing so, partly having regard to the official position of her husband.

I should, perhaps, remark here that I have never claimed for hypnotism, even if backed by the best of other treatment, that it is a panacea for all complaints, or even for all cases of a single type. Nevertheless, many seemingly incurable cases rapidly recover by means of the measures I advocate.

A German lady, a Bachelor of Civil and Canon law, sought my aid. She was about fifty years of age, and when about fifteen had the toes of both feet smashed by a fall. The resulting deformity and later debility gave rise to Raynaud's Disease. "Being declared incurable by some practitioners, and not consenting to have all the toes amputated," she wrote, "I finally accepted an eminent surgeon's advice to have two toes cut off for the sake of helping the others." *My* help included manipulation of the whole of the toes, and daily vegetable stews, and, on the day appointed for the operation, she walked to the hospital as a surprise for the surgeon!

Another patient who suffered from Raynaud's Disease was a lady who had had half a finger amputated, and in whom the complaint was spreading. In this instance I used hypnotic suggestion and prescribed a diet mainly raw and almost sugarless. No recurrence of the Raynaud's Disease occurred—and I was in touch with this lady five years after the recovery.

Out of gratitude, the second patient sent to me another supposed sufferer from the complaint. However, it was not Raynaud's Disease but Ergotism, a result of a medical man having attempted to cure excessive menstruation by dosing with ergot. The patient was then sixteen years of age, and the doctoring lasted six months. Shortly after, one of her fingers came away into a bandage. When, at rather more than thirty years of age, she was sent to me, her hands were a mass of stumps, and her mentality was not of the best. She did not adhere to my advice, but had she acted differently I doubt whether she would have recovered. That occurred a short time before I returned south from Northumberland, about the end of 1924. The lady died a year or two later. Her case was not the only one from which I have known dire results to occur from dosing with ergot.

Not infrequently, rheumatoid arthritis can be arrested and the health of the erstwhile sufferer restored by my procedures. A clergyman wrote to me: "I feel I must write to you to express my great appreciation of the treatment that I have undergone at your hands. My rheumatism, which had troubled me from childhood—*i.e.* about forty years—was promptly cured, a result which I considered impossible of achievement. . . . I believe I have mentioned to you that I have four times had rheumatic fever with heart complications. You have made me as fit as a proverbial fiddle."

That clergyman, when last I heard of him, was nearly approaching his ninetieth year.

When lecturing at Denham in April 1934, I had as chairman the Principal of a public school in the vicinity, and he "spoke" (stated the *Harrow Observer*) "of the 'veritable miracle' performed by Mr. Orton in curing him, within two months, of various disabilities connected with œdema" (dropsy) "of the brain and lungs, and which had lasted several years despite the many medical specialists consulted."

"A member of the audience" (continued the account) "volunteered a statement regarding his own immediate abandonment of glasses through Mr. Orton's help, and also Mr. Orton's cure of bronchial catarrh of so serious a nature that his physician" (a local M.D.) "had said that, without rest and extreme care he would probably end his days in a consumption sanatorium. A few months after the verdict he was insured by the Norwich Union Insurance Company as a first class life."

Those few cases are chosen almost at random, and are by no means exceptional. Unless I can see a likelihood of cure or amelioration, I never undertake the case, and I have never lost a client by death, nor sent that client away as safer to die elsewhere. "The faith that is in me" was founded on just foundations, and has been confirmed by success, whereas "qualified" medical men do not agree on even fundamentals of theory or practice. With wide diversity of medical opinions, it is indispensable, up to a point, to judge for oneself—just as "qualified" practitioners are apt to consider themselves justified in doing. Acting on that principle, I have been enabled to help the medical profession itself. Medical men of high standing have been and are pleased to acknowledge their indebtedness to my achievements in the medical field; they have used some of my methods, have sent to me patients whom they were unable to help, and have even come to me, themselves, for treatment and tuition. Whatever evidences of professional jealousy I may have experienced in certain instances, I have no just cause to feel animosity towards medical men as a body—that would be ungracious and ungrateful. Whatever I may have accomplished in the medical field would have been all but impossible but for the labours of predecessors, many of whom were qualified practitioners. And to the living, I am in many cases deeply indebted.

CHAPTER XIV

MENTAL AND NERVOUS COMPLAINTS.

When persons come to me complaining that their nerves are out of order, they rarely describe their trouble correctly, their whole system being at fault. Such persons probably complain of a worrying disposition, of a tendency to timidity, of depression, irresolution, languor, insomnia, and loss of memory and the power of "concentration," and very likely tell me that they have employed various supposed remedies, but without good result. In many cases these persons have expected "medicine" to take the place of adherence to the laws of health. The truth of the matter is that in many cases hypnotism cannot by itself effect a *cure*, and needs to be supplemented by other helps to well-being. Even when people seem to have a mental trouble without a physical, the appearance is apt to be misleading; and similarly, when trouble is supposed to be purely physical a mental element is usually present.

The average person does not pay due attention to health requirements, and, indeed, rarely knows them. When, therefore, a trouble comes, its effect is intensified and, frequently, the inclination to battle with it is lost. The condition of the brain reacts on digestion and the body-functions generally, and the organism thereby becomes more and more debilitated. The mind is thus made a fertile soil for absurd fears and obsessions, and the trouble sometimes progresses to melancholia or acute mania.

Sometimes the forerunners of serious "nervous" trouble are clear, at other times skill is required to detect them. The dangerous condition of the brain is that in which there is an insensibility of ill, and, therefore, no tendency to lessen or relinquish labour. On the other hand, there may be a sense of weight on the top of the head—not a head*ache*—or a feeling of tightness about the forehead; there may be sleeplessness, loss of control over certain groups of muscles, numbness of the extremities, failure of memory, momentary loss of consciousness, and lack of the power of continued attention.

In my eighth chapter I referred to the harm wrought by strained attempts to stifle an emotion. The remarks there made have a strong bearing upon the matter now under consideration.

In some military hospitals nerve patients were told to try to forget their trouble and nasty experiences; whilst in other military hospitals they were told to talk about them as much as they could. Apparently the second direction was by far the better. Why? Because in the first instance men were prone to say: "I shall try hard to forget that occurrence, but I'm afraid" (or "sure") "I shall not succeed;" whereas in the second instance the men would probably say: "Talking about my troubles will help to cure me." They did not stifle the disagreeable ideas, and perhaps they had forgotten part, but, by association it was likely to arise and be looked at closely. Thus, familiarity would breed contempt.

It became much the same with them as with some men who got over their fear of blood when at the front. Indeed, the imagination of a " horror " may be far worse than the reality. Usually, the best way to overcome fear is to look in the face that of which we are afraid.

In the hospital instances to which I have referred there was at first a mental *conflict*, a disinclination to face reality. That is the underlying cause of many of the puzzling peculiarities of neurotics.

The word " neurotic " does not imply that the sufferer is lacking common-sense or sanity. Like a hypochondriac or hysteric, a neurotic is perfectly well aware that his fears are unreasonable, incapable though he may seem to banish or to explain them.

The mental trouble of a neurotic may be characterised by morbid anxieties (*neuroses*) or by hysterical symptoms (*psychoses*). The latter class can hardly be explained without taking into consideration mental experiences of the sufferer's childhood, results of which experiences remain. Because so much of early life is forgotten, the assumption is apt to be made that the mental *impressions* are *completely* obliterated, but that conclusion is wrong.

Nervous characteristics must not be confused with " nerviness "; a person of nervous constitution when in good health is usually energetic and capable, and quite free from neurotic tendencies or silly fears.

Nevertheless, Napoleon Bonaparte, Wellington and Lord Roberts displayed marked nervous symptoms whenever a cat entered the room. Among not altogether dissimilar sufferers who have procured my assistance are generals and judges.

One lady who came to me to be freed of a fear of committing suicide explained that her inclination had been so great that she had wisely taken the precaution of putting all bottles containing poison so high that they were out of her reach!

Nurture amidst phantasies is the source of much mental and nervous trouble. Women are more prone than are men to phantasies in adult life, consequently a large proportion of them are more or less neurotic.

Sometimes girls have been fussed by their fathers, but kept ignorant of sex-matters. When they married they were shocked by their marital experiences—and thus neurotic symptoms arose. Being straight-laced is a frequent cause of nervous trouble.

Sir Frederick Mott showed to me a collection of interesting photographs illustrating a variety of war-cases that, for a long time, were supposed by reputable medical practitioners to be organic in character, and were treated accordingly, but were nevertheless cured by him almost immediately. His methods included indirect suggestion, but also much that is generally included under the term "psycho-analysis." At the same time he widely disagreed with the theories put forward by Professor Freud of Vienna, the apparent originator of that term, and I was gratified to find that as regards theory the conclusions drawn by the English neurologist and by myself bore a close resemblance.

It has been contended that the term "psycho-analysis" should be confined to Freudian psychology; that neither those who taking Freud's ideas as a basis of their own investigations and who develop them in a different direction, nor persons who have incorporated other theories with those of Freud, are entitled to make use of the term "psycho-analysis." Certainly Freud acted in the manner advocated, his theories being modifications, extensions and corruptions of those of Professor Pierre Janet, who called his own system "psychological analysis." Janet, I maintain, was considerably nearer the truth than was Freud, even since the latter made those modifications of his theory which include giving up his previous claim that all fear is of sexual origin—battle-dreams, for example, having convinced him of that error. It is mainly in connection with Freud's sexual interpretation of dreams and impulses that his views obtained much publicity. But independent of battle-dreams, and similar considerations, the absurdity of Freud's contention that all fear is of neurotic character and should be attributed to suppression of sexual impulses ought to be obvious to anyone acquainted with infants and animals—say, for example, cats! In short, though within psycho-analytic literature there is some useful material, there is much that is definitely harmful, tending to undermine the mental fabric instead of restoring it to a condition of stability. By Freud and others facts have been distorted and muddled, and the results made premises from which to draw unwarranted and ridiculous conclusions.

A large proportion of what goes under the name " psycho-analysis " is a mixture of direct and indirect suggestion. The operator's statement, so often made, that he does not use suggestion, and does not hold with it, is equivalent to saying that the *procedures* he employs have a particular value; but such a value as many of them have, corresponds exactly with that of a bread-and-sugar pill in which confidence is placed by the patient. However, the patient very likely would not believe in a pill for mental ills, whereas he or she may believe that psycho-analysis is a genuine remedy.

Nevertheless, in many cases the use of hypnotism as merely a suitable condition for suggestive treatment is radically wrong. Before putting suggestions into, or before, a mind the operator should endeavour to gauge the nature of the proposed receptacle and what it already contains. Suggestions may not only be misunderstood, they may create or increase conflict in the mind of the patient.

Attempts made whilst the sufferer is in the " normal " state to discover hidden mental causes of his or her condition may be entirely useless, though likely to involve much time and expense. The best way of dealing with the matter is first to induce hypnosis.

In 1889 Janet pointed out: " The final somnambulistic state " (by which he meant " deep hypnosis ") " is a state in which the subject, no matter how depressed and sick he may be in the waking state, becomes quite identical with the individual in his best and most normal condition."

There was a time when many doctors were wont to refer to hypnotism as a form of hysteria, and to the possible forgetfulness upon " awakening " as evidence. I pointed out, long ago, that such persons overlook the fact that the loss of recollection (the hysterical element if such there be) belongs to normal life. The capacity of recollection during hypnosis is much greater than during the " normal " condition; it comprehends the normal and some (usually much) additional material—even when the hypnosis is but light. Consistent, too, with what Janet stated, psychasthenic and most other stammerers and stutterers rarely show their defect when they are hypnotised. Hysteria is concerned with *loss* of control as regards one's own organism, hypnosis with a corresponding *gain*.

The unhypnotised person may be out of touch with required memories, whereas the hypnotised person is in close touch, even when the hypnosis is not profound. Persons in hypnosis, too, can in any case more vividly recall a circumstance; and that is another advantage, for the more strongly the events are recalled, the more strongly is experienced the emotional element connected with them.

To exemplify the significance of the procedures I here advocate, I will refer to just one of many similar cases of my own. In this instance the cause of a trouble had been forgotten in " normal " life and the trouble itself persisted through suggestion solely. The patient had reached manhood. During an illness of early childhood his tonsils were removed by a callous doctor; and the child became a stammerer and stutterer, and did not recover until he recollected the origin of his complaint, realised how the trouble arose, and decided that its continuance was unnecessary.

In general, the neurotic should be led to understand himself. Sometimes he may himself unravel the skein of his emotional life; sometimes he needs just a little help—not so much telling as hinting; sometimes a story of some other case will make him see himself as he is, laugh at himself, make new resolves, and recover.

In his book, *La Médicine Psychologique,* Dr. Pierre Janet goes so far as to assert: "People will progressively come to understand that the types of mental maladies we consider as real madness are only different degrees of a trouble which has passed through all sorts of evolutions, and the germ of which was present in disharmonies of the character. It will be easy to understand that if we modify these first degrees of psychological weakness we shall stop the development of more serious forms. Most mental diseases are curable, in a high proportion of cases, during the first stages of the affection."

The quoted statement reminds us of the existence of mental hygiene, of which the procedures advocated in this work are important parts.

. . . .

Sometimes, on the principle that "the greater includes the less," profound changes of mental attitude are procurable. An experiment, undertaken with a Mrs. G. M. Fowler, described as a "thirty-one-year-old married woman," was thus referred to in the *Daily Mirror* of 25th October, 1934:—

"An amazed crowd of mechanics and pilots at Hanworth Airport yesterday saw her put into a hypnotic trance by Mr. J. Louis Orton . . . . . as she sat in the cockpit of the machine. *Then, accompanied by Mr. Orton, she went up in the air, piloted by Mr. Duncanson, a Hanworth pilot. She exhibited no signs of fear during the whole of the flight.*" (The aeroplane ascended 4,500 feet.) "After she had stepped out of the machine and been de-hypnotised, Mrs. Fowler told the *Daily Mirror*: 'I have always had a fear of heights, possibly because, when an infant, I hated being thrown into the air. At nine years old I was enticed to ride on a scenic railway. I screamed with sheer dread during the entire ride. When I read about the air race to Australia I said I could never face air travel; but I have such faith in Mr. Orton's powers that I finally consented to try this experiment. *While in the air, I was able to pick out objects on the ground below, which is quite possible when in a trance. Now I shall never again be afraid to make a flight.*' Mr. Orton, who claims that this is the first experiment of its kind in relation of hypnotism and aviation, said: '. . . In the case of Mrs. Fowler, the nervousness of ascending heights was not dissipated *prior* to the experiment. I am anxious that hypnotism should be recognised as perfectly harmless, and not a conflict between two minds.'"

The Stage, of 8th November, 1934, declared: "Since the publication of Mrs. Fowler's hypnotic excursion, I have heard a well-known playwright declare that he will call upon Mr. Orton's powers on the first night of his next play, to find out experimentally if hypnotism will dispel the tortures he goes through on such occasions."

That playwright made a wise decision.

The *Middlesex Advertiser,* in reporting a lecture and demonstration which I gave under the auspices of the Anglo-American Radio and Television Society, on the 31st October, 1934, stated:—

"Mr. Louis Orton referred to the aviation-and-hypnotism experiments he was conducting. He emphasised that he was approaching hypnotism from a new angle, but one which makes palpable the use of hypnotism for the overcoming of fears of certain varieties. . . . He said that his experiments had a strong bearing upon voice-culture, inasmuch as stage-fright and similar handicaps were parts of what is sometimes described as an 'inferiority complex.' He emphasised that the dissipation of 'silly' fears does not usually necessitate, despite the misrepresentations of psychoanalysts, a discovery of the memories associated with the fears in the first place. All that is actually requisite is a favourable alteration of mental attitude. Indeed, said the lecturer, elaborate means employed ostensibly for the purpose of discovery often lead to worse troubles than they are intended to remove. Achievement which gives confidence carries many advantages alongside as his experiments evidenced. For that reason, achievement through the help of hypnotic suggestion supplies the key to the situation. . . . The great end of hypnotism as employed by an expert is the raising of the mental level, so that what was unusual, or 'impossible,' becomes usual and a source of achievement in whatever direction a person's talents are used."

A very gratifying sequel occurred in reference to the account in the *Daily Mirror*. A celebrated man, unfortunately a drunkard, had decided, owing to domestic troubles, to commit suicide by putting his head in the gas-oven. He had actually turned on the taps; then he suddenly remembered the cutting which he had made, as a curiosity, from the newspaper mentioned. He turned off the taps, went to his bureau, found the cutting, got into touch with me, was treated by hypnotism, and was cured in a single visit of his drunkenness, of his despondency, and of their dire tendencies.

CHAPTER XV

MORAL REFORM

THAT much criminality proceeds from tumours on the brain, and from defects at birth, seems well established; also that in some instances cure of vice can be effected by operation. But equally well established is the fact that by means of hypnotic treatment a large proportion of criminals, especially young ones, can be reclaimed.

The Italian savant, Professor Lombroso, claimed to have discovered a criminal type, the "instinctive" or "born" criminal. Much publicity was given to his views, and he obtained a large following. However, despite the propagandist literature that ensued, Lombroso's views were shown to be as unreliable on the matter as were those he expressed regarding the supposed neurotic origin of genius. As regards the alleged criminal type, he laid great stress on certain physiognomical peculiarities. Someone present at an important meeting where the matter was discussed aptly pointed out that those peculiarities were peculiarities of scientists present.

The truth is that the faces of criminals are apt to show evidences of recklessness, weariness and misery—and even may suggest, in some instances, scarcity of that useful commodity, soap. The so-called "hardened criminal," however, is surely not the worst sinner necessarily. The detected criminal may be incautious and weak-minded; and there are many persons about who, either through their own skill or that of others, evade the law, may carry on a career of sheer bluff, and at heart be brutal.

Lombroso's conclusions were drawn from a deficient number and variety of cases; therefore it occurred that very soon there was wide disagreement between the favourers of supposed anatomical criminology, which now has few upholders. Still, the questions raised through the investigation had one excellent effect; they riveted attention on the underlying causes of crime, and therefore stimulated inquiry as to the most thorough and practicable ways of dealing with them.

Among reforming agents hypnotism must be given a prominent place. It does not *create* characteristics, but it can, and does, reveal and develop them—even in cases where they were deemed non-existent. At the same time I ought to point out that there are limitations to the use of hypnotism in moral culture—just as in physical and intellectual. Indeed, some cases of immorality betoken extreme mental obtusity. A man who had been blind since birth, and therefore was without any experience of sight, expressed the opinion that the colour red must resemble the sound of a trumpet. Similarly, there are, or seem to be, persons blind *morally* having only one conception of virtue—namely, as of some weakness from which they pride themselves, upon being free. For such persons, if such exist, there can be no hope of moral reformation in thought—though perhaps in action. Such persons are certainly no more than an extreme minority, and it is only with great reluctance that I have even hinted at the existence of such moral obtusity as they seem to display. As to the extent of whatever good slumbers in a human character, who is entitled to be positive?

One of the greatest obstacles to the success of moral reformation through hypnotism is reluctance on the part of subjects to relinquish pet sins. Obviously, if a subject is capable of refusing *from mere caprice* to comply with a commonplace suggestion (and every subject can thus refuse), it can hardly be expected that he will be willing to throw aside, without realising what he or she considers ample recompense, a mode of conduct viewed as highly advantageous. Nevertheless, where there is an obviously tender spot to work upon, much good can be effected.

Not infrequently the moral sense is badly in need of enlightenment. The story is told—I do not vouch for its truth—of a cannibal chief who had resolved upon the killing and eating of a missionary. The latter remonstrated, insisting that the proposed conduct was wicked. But the cannibal was far from convinced. "I reverence the memory of my mother," said he, "and the last time I saw her she was propped up against a tree, eating cold missionary."

Perhaps that story is unlikely to be true! However, here is another story, and in this case a true one. A traveller among the cannibal natives of New Guinea remonstrated with one who was assisting to eat his mother's corpse. His retort was to the point: "Why waste good meat?" he asked. I seriously think the implications of that story are worth reflecting upon. The cannibal was no doubt correct who remarked that "tastes differ." When I visited Salt Lake City, a married niece of Heber J. Grant, the President of the Mormon Church, told me that, even had polygamy still been practised by members of her church, she would not have been "saintly enough" to have consented to be one among wives of a man—she would have been too jealous!

"Hypnotic suggestion," wrote the celebrated Swiss mental specialist, Professor August Forel, "is a sovereign remedy for acquired bad habits." Suggestion in some form, I would add, is indispensable. The prevalence of alcoholism and drug addiction has given rise to the exploitation of almost innumerable "remedies." For alcoholism bromide of potassium has been employed extensively. Sodium bi-carbonate is the main ingredient of another powder, whilst other powders contain atropine, hyocine, or some other poisonous drug. One ostensible remedy consists of injecting under the skin "Croton water!" And for the cure of the drug habit hypodermic injections of one or other stimulating—or more correctly irritating—drug has been employed—usually strychnine, atropine, cannabis indica, or hyoscyamine. With these ostensible remedies is always coupled the assertion that the patient will be cured of the habit if he follow directions; and cure, when it does occur, is the outcome of confidence in that assertion. By the substitution of an inert powder for the drug, or the injection of pure water—of course provided the ruse be undiscovered by the patient—the result is even better, because no counteracting injury has been caused to the organism.

In some instances, especially of the drug habit, a special arrangement of the patient's diet is a valuable adjunct to hypnotic treatment, particularly as the poison imbibed tends to make suggestive treatment difficult. Nevertheless, though violence and lust are often looked upon as common characteristics of dipsomaniacs, and cowardice of morphinomaniacs, these bad qualities are often the outcome in a great measure of unintentional auto-suggestion or expectation. Further, many persons believe themselves slaves of a habit when as yet they are only slaves of the fear. Such persons are usually curable quickly and permanently.

Nobody chooses to do evil for the sake of its being evil. The temptation consists in the fact that the performance of the action either affords, or seems to promise, some pleasure or benefit to its perpetrator, or that he believes that he has not the power to resist the inclination. Hypnotic treatment that is skilful aims at making the delinquent realise why his or her conduct is self-defeating, and of instilling confidence in the ability to resist—without a struggle—future temptations. With a person thus treated, alongside future temptation comes a vivid realisation of the right conduct to be pursued.

Sex-troubles of many varieties, and troubles indirectly connected with sex—often unrecognised as such by the sufferers—require, for swift and yet permanent treatment, psychological treatment in which hypnotism plays a vitally important part. I should, however, add that I have abundant evidence that much harm is wrought by so-called " purity " books that misrepresent and exaggerate. Though some few youthful readers of such books are only too well aware of their unreliability, and may consequently carry to serious lengths the results of their scepticism, there are many persons in whom needless or disproportionate fears are aroused, fears which, nevertheless, may exercise a baneful influence throughout life. I speak from very wide experience when I say that, in administering treatment, the best results are obtained by steering clear of humbug and rigidly adhering to the truth. I do not aim at duping my subjects into the acceptance of a stereotyped " purity," but strive to make them look at matters in a rational light. I find that to be the surest means of establishing *genuine* morality.

Occasionally I have been called upon to cure kleptomania. By some the idea of that complaint is scouted; but that it actually exists is provable by the fact that it can be cured. The distinction between thieving proper and kleptomania is that the thief steals from a motive, the kleptomaniac either without one or through fancying that voices demand the appropriation of certain articles. An ordinary kleptomaniac happening to glance at a bunch of keys may almost unconsciously pocket them as if for security. Upon the missing articles being inquired about, by association of ideas he may recollect the whole occurrence and hasten to explain. Sufferers of that nature can readily be cured by hypnotism; and, despite what some writers have declared to the contrary, I doubt whether kleptomania is ever heritable—it may arise through the *idea* that it " runs in the family."

Many persons have come to me to be cured of inveterate smoking, in some instances after having tried auto-suggestion unsuccessfully for years; yet, almost without exception, cure has been immediate. To one of these persons I added the suggestion that he would refrain from indulgence in sweet things prone to affect his voice unfavourably and to lead to colds. The suggestion as to smoking was complied with, that as to diet ignored. The individual had had post-hypnotic amnesia, and was surprised when I told him that he was passionately fond of sweet things. He admitted that the statement was true, adding that he would be very unwilling to part with his " sweet tooth," though aware that it was a disadvantage. " Well, in that case," I said, " you would not mind giving up the articles, but the taste." He laughingly agreed, and I therefore suggested that in future sweet articles would to him taste bitter, and bitter articles sweet. The suggestion was completely successful, and the result permanent.

Once I was asked to treat by hypnotism a lady who accused herself of being a glutton and an inveterate nail-biter. Convinced that the " gluttony " was merely a hearty, healthy appetite, I refrained from giving the lady suggestions that might have had bad, and even disastrous, results; I suggested, whilst the lady was in hypnosis, that she would not eat beyond the extent necessary to supply abundant energy. As regards the nail-biting, I was more acquiescent; I hypnotically suggested the immediate abandonment of the habit. The results of the treatment were thus described in a letter I received a few months later:—

"I have been thinking you might be interested to hear how I got on since my treatment. Well—the nail-biting has magically ceased! Wonderful it is how a habit of nearly sixty years should stop in a moment! But, alas, the gluttony has not been overcome. . . . It amazes me how simple your treatment was—I must confess I was a little disappointed! I had hoped to be put into a trance or some such, was curious to know what it felt like! Anyhow, it did the trick as far as the nail-biting is concerned and probably would have stopped the gluttony too had you stressed it more." A few years had passed when the lady wrote to me again. She informed me that the cure of nail-biting had proved to be complete and permanent.

Whoever has grasped the true nature of hypnotism must realise how serious an error is the reservation of hypnotism until all other known means of possible reformation have been tried and failed. Numerous instances in my experience testify to the fact that such a neglect of hypnotism has meant the loss of valuable years of progress, and not infrequently, of health too. Whatever can be said of the value of hypnotism for helping students out of difficulties of an intellectual nature, can be said with equal truth in reference to the hypnotic moulding of character. The parent who declared that he would rather have his child *naturally* bad than *hypnotically* good, might, with equal sense—

or nonsense—have said that he would rather have his child ignorant than educated. Punitive methods may be a deterrent to some extent, but, in effect, that is lopping at the branches of the tree of crime instead of getting at its root. Bishop Hurd well said that the young should be prepared to see the world without surprise, and live in it without danger. Without the aid of hypnotism that end can hardly be attained or approached with anything like certainty; whereas, by the skilful and persistent employment of hypnotism in every schoolroom, the reformatories would ere long be almost wholly deprived of new inmates; and, if similarly employed in the reformatories, more than fifty per cent. of vicious children could be reclaimed.

Comparatively few persons become habitual criminals when under sixteen years of age or over twenty-one. As matters now stand, from lack of the help that could readily be given by hypnotism, many a life is doomed to shipwreck—many a person who might have led a useful existence becomes and remains a criminal.

CHAPTER XVI

EDUCATIONAL AND SOCIAL USES

READERS of my book, *Memory Efficiency*, can scarcely fail to realise that there is absolutely no valid reason for believing—notwithstanding Cannon's declarations and fantastic stories to the contrary—that a child is conscious before it is born. Reflection is but gradually brought to bear in infancy, and, as the incidents of early post-natal life make scarcely any impression on the mind of the infant, it is clear that pre-natal life cannot be more understanding. Nevertheless, the early impressions of childhood exercise a profound and far-reaching influence on the mentality.

Sir John A. Cockburn, in speaking at an educational congress at University College, London, on the 5th of January, 1925, emphasised the importance of realisation, on the part of parents, that in even a supposedly ordinary child there is a spark of genius, that often that spark is quenched, but if allowed to grow into a flame, astonishing results may occur in later life. "Above all," said Sir John, "the parent must avoid making fingermarks upon the delicate tissues of the child's mind. The whole mechanism of the child's brain may be spoiled before ever it comes into the hands of the teachers."

One can go still further back. Though ascribed pre-natal impressions are in general fictitious, there is abundant evidence to support the contention that an expectant mother may so harbour unhealthy thoughts as to cause peculiar mental tendencies, and even physical peculiarities, in the coming child. As pointed out, with details, in my book on *Personality*, the troubles usually considered all but inseparable from pregnancy and childbirth are partly due to wrong feeding especially, and partly to suggestion; and in the main are curable—therefore preventable. Expectant mothers can also have almost assured that great joy of motherhood—the suckling of the infant.

Adults are prone to ignore the effect upon their own minds of passing circumstances. But how the desires of childhood differ from those of adult life! The elements that make the adult mind were in the mind of the child.

"Actions speak louder than words," says an old adage. A child is far more likely to follow an example than an abstract idea; therefore, before parents should blame their children for faults, they should examine their own conduct, which may, perchance, have been the cause.

As regards sex (and other) matters, I should lay down this rule: When a child is old enough to ask a question, he or she is old enough to be answered truthfully.

A child scarcely owes a debt of gratitude to its parents *because* they brought it into the world; that is where the parents' obligations come in. Further, a child should hardly be expected to really honour, much less love, its parents, unless they give it cause.

A child may reason very well from the knowledge it has, but the earliest steps in education cannot be made by means of reasoning. Nevertheless, as early as practicable, children should be encouraged to reason, but they should be shown how incorrect conclusions can arise through the assumption of wrong premises. Suggestion should be used to guide the imagination and emotions, but never to influence unfairly the child's mind.

By the time a child reaches school-days, its mental characteristics have usually taken a decided bent. The duty of a teacher is to do for his or her pupils what they cannot do for themselves, and what they cannot do without the expenditure of too much time and energy. Children should be led to reflect, to judge, and to act, for themselves; but that they may perform those duties well, they need the use of their whole mental outfit—which includes familiarity with the contemplative, as well as with the observative, mood. Much has been written of late years as regards allowing "freedom" to schoolchildren. I should be much surprised if it transpired that the opinions of the pupils of the teachers concerned did not bear a striking resemblance on religious and other matters. I am a whole-hearted believer in freedom, and, in order that each human being should have as much as possible, should like to see knowledge give power through re-education of the neglected functions.

Precocity is usually too hasty development—which circumstance explains why so few persons who, as infants, were prodigies, fulfil in adult life their apparent promise. On the other hand, it is noteworthy that many of the world's greatest men were considered as children quite ordinary—or even exceptionally stupid. Newton, when a boy, occupied for some time the bottom of the lowest form in the school he attended. David Hume, Richard Brinsley Sheridan, Thomas Moore (the Irish poet), and Sir Walter Scott were considered blockheads by their mothers. Particular difficulty was found by "George Eliot" in learning to read. Molière, at fourteen years of age, could barely read and write. Pestalozzi, Howard, Wellington, Coleridge, Balzac, and I believe Kitchener, were considered, when at school, "dunces." Rossini and Wagner were regarded as idiots by their fellow-pupils. Dean Swift, Göethe, and Tolstoi were refused their degrees because they failed in their university examinations. Verdi was rejected, as even a paying pupil, at the Milan Conservatorio. Diderot was looked upon as the shame of his family. Goldsmith was thought to be a stupid child. Theodore Parker, when a youth, apparently had but poor powers of recollection, but eventually had learned thirty-four languages.

It is often by an apparently trivial, often by what seems to be an unfortunate, incident that obscured powers become evident. It was the eloquence of Callistratus which inspired Demosthenes with the resolve to become an orator. Milton lost his position as secretary to Cromwell, and that led to his writing *Paradise Lost*. Shakespeare fled from his native county in consequence of some juvenile errors, became an actor, and thus a playwright. Considering the extraordinary gifts thus revealed, as it were by accident, should it be wondered at if aptitudes of far less brilliance often remain latent?

How many persons fail in consequence of the lack

of some one or other quality! If confidence, for example, be lacking, a student, however gifted, is unlikely to persevere, and, even with perseverance, is foiled of completest success; without perseverance the greatest gifts are obscured—and the same is true regarding " concentration." The quickest and best way of acquiring "concentration" is by means of hypnotic processes. Then (by utilising that " concentration ") memory, observation, and the other attributes essential to success are rapidly developed. " A chain is as strong only as its weakest link "; hypnotism strengthens not only the weakest link, but all the links in the educational chain, and therefore it leads not only from failure to success, but from moderate success to much greater, and to all students it proves an incalculable time-saver.

Hypnosis is the best possible condition for study, being, as I have shown, identical with the fruitful contemplative mood for which genius is so celebrated. In genius, unfortunately, there is often too great a tendency to contemplation and too little self-control and prudent attention to one's worldly interests. May I repeat that hypnotism tends to form, and often forms (extemporises, if you like), *balanced* genius (?).

Through the agency of hypnotism the student may be enabled to have a ready hold on much of the knowledge previously obtained, to increase rapidly the available store of knowledge, to utilise more quickly, though more thoroughly, what he knows, to isolate or combine movements readily, and to be happy in his work.

A famous novelist, defeated temporarily by his own technique, wrote to me after one visit: " My ideas are taking form like negatives under a developer," and later: "For myself, your treatment early in 1943 worked a miracle so far as my literary activities are concerned. Ideas are now twelve a penny, and my notebooks are crammed to capacity."

The powers of remembrance during deep hypnosis are so extraordinary that some investigators have jumped to the unwarranted conclusion that not only the impressions made by events leave a trace, but that the actual memory of all actions and states of consciousness is recoverable by hypnotism. However, I have obtained evidence of the genuineness of what were ostensibly remembrances of even the first year of life. The subject of one such experiment I conducted described hypnotism aptly as a "memory *tonic*." Certainly in that connection it is unequalled in efficacy. A typical instance was that of a lady, a medical student, who had employed auto-suggestion so ineffectively on the first of four days' examination that she sought my aid privately. The next day she was surprised to find that of forty *viva voce* questions, the right answers to thirty-nine sprang into consciousness immediately; and at the end of the examination, despite the one unsatisfactory day, her name stood at the top of the list, with 90 per cent. of the possible marks. On the 10th September, 1928, there were reported to the British Association at Glasgow particulars of Cambridge men who had been hypnotised before examinations and had then passed with flying colours. They had been told during hypnosis that "they would be able to do everything they wanted to do more easily, accurately, and quickly than ever before." These students were treated twice a week for two or three months before the examination. In my own experience (since 1901) rarely has a student required more than a few treatments; often one treatment sufficed. I have had but a single failure; and he could not recollect what he had never known.

Conversely, by hypnotic suggestion, undesirable recollections, *e.g.,* of disastrous love affairs, can in many cases be crowded or blotted out.

On many occasions I have been appealed to, usually successfully, for the rectification, through hypnotic and allied treatment, of marital and other love affairs that had gone awry.

Happiness is largely dependent upon health and success, and, as I have attempted to show, hypnotism is a potent aid to the attainment of both. But for trouble of all kinds, it often proves an efficient remedy. "He who does not find ease in himself," wrote La Rochefoucault, "seeks for it in vain elsewhere." The instances in which, by means of hypnotism, I have procured fortitude in trying situations—*e.g.*, during the illness and at the deathbed of a dearly-beloved relative—have been many. On some occasions I have turned the patient's attention from the thought of trouble to that of work, which became in turn a comforting friend. In cases of fright, shyness, diffidence, and similar handicaps, whether in children or adults, I have usually found hypnotic treatment an efficient remedy.

Sometimes absurd claims are made respecting the practice of hypnotism as a factor conducive to professional and business success; but, stripped of all exaggeration, the aptitudes and study necessary to make a good hypnotist are such as, in ordinary life, are well calculated to win the confidence and (I venture to add) the esteem of one's fellows. Further, in very many instances persons have told me that what they have gained through being treated for the instilling of self-confidence and perseverance has greatly affected their ordinary avocation—they have become successes. Now, what applies there to the subject must surely apply to the operator. Indeed, as a general rule, whether one is a success or failure depends far more on the way in which external events are viewed than upon their actual nature. Allow me to emphasise that, whoever you may be, in all likelihood much of your mental power is latent. and that without the requisitioning of that latent power you are handicapped in all your intellectual endeavours. Hypnotism, when used conscientiously and expertly, can ensure getting into closer touch with the treasures which you hold within you, can supplement those possessions, and can help you to succeed in directions where possibly, or even probably, you have never dared to press. There are but few persons who, in the estimate they make regarding their innate abilities, do not hold themselves "too cheap."

As an aid to all-round success and to happiness, hypnotism can be of inestimable value, and therefore the day is bound to come, sooner or later, when it will take its place in the generally-accepted curriculum. As regards the present, it is the obvious duty of those who recognise and have experienced its value, to press it before the notice of the general public. *We want the best, and we want it now.*

CHAPTER XVII

MUSIC AND VOICE

THROUGH adversity, the eventually great pianist and composer, Rachmaninoff, had sunk into a condition of fearful apathy. He had promised to write a concerto, but for two years " did nothing ", lying on a couch all day he preferred the company of his dog to that of human kind. Eventually the importunities of some young friends led him to seek the aid of Dr. Dahl, who at that time was celebrated for " magic " cures. Day after day Rachmaninoff reposed in an armchair, whilst Dahl brought to bear hypnotic verbal suggestion. " You will begin to write your concerto . . . . You will work with great facility. . . . The concerto will be of excellent quality." " It was always the same, without interruption," Rachmaninoff told von Riesemann. " Although it may sound incredible, this cure really helped me. Already I began again to compose. The material grew in bulk, and new musical ideas began to stir within me—far more than I needed for my concerto."

The concerto proved a great success, and was dedicated to Dr. Dahl, " out of gratitude."

Extreme sensibility is common to all artistic minds and is prone to lead to nervousness which never is helpful in itself, and which, when persisting in the presence of audiences, inevitably mars performance—hurrying the action of the heart and respiratory organs, thus making the voice of the singer spasmodic and uncertain and the fingers of the instrumentalist unresponsive, besides seriously interfering with memory and the extent of needed expression. In such instances, hypnotic procedure can often prove a friend indeed! The erstwhile nervy and self-conscious performer can be enabled to procure absorption in the performance itself—an essential to faithful exhibition of intrinsic beauties and delicacies. I have dealt successfully with pianists, players of string and wind instruments, and other musicians prone to the "jitters."

Almost for a century investigators have attempted to bring hypnotic procedures to bear in connection with musical, vocal and histrionic art. In my book, *Rational Hypnotism,* I have quoted details concerning a variety of interesting and suggestive experiments of the kind. Such instances show that even in the hands of an operator deficient in knowledge of the particular subjects concerned, hypnotism can be productive of good effects. A factory girl, whilst hypnotised by Braid, performed before Jenny Lind some feats of phonic imitation (in song and speech) that would doubtless be astonishing to persons unacquainted with a certain class of hypnotic phenomena. Braid wrongly imagined that the girl could not be enabled to retain the ability for use apart from specific hypnotism. Imagination (as in her case) and design (usually for advertising and sensational purposes) are the only obstacles. Realising in some measure that important fact, Dr. Quackenbos (a professor Emeritus of Columbia University), Dr. Osgood Mason and others have employed hypnotic artifices for instilling self-confidence, perseverance, and the like, and, in general, their results were of more utility than were Braid's. Nevertheless, hazy and erroneous notions regarding the nature of hypnotism, and partial or complete ignorance regarding genuine voice culture, rendered their labours in this connection one-sided and misleading.

Many years ago an organist, who came to me to be taught singing, expressed the opinion that really good voices were rare among the boys of his neighbourhood. "A short time ago," he said, by way of exemplification, "I took in hand about twenty boys in order to find suitable voices for vacancies in my choir. Twice or more a week I took the boys through some exercises. At the end of a month there were only three or four boys any good, all the other voices had given way under training." Alas! That organist did not then know (though he soon learned) that voice culture, truly so called, does not consist of haphazard scale singing. Consider his case and then you cannot fail to realise that though a competent hypnotist can "inspire" those he treats to do the best they know how, he cannot impart to them technical knowledge of which *he himself is ignorant*, and that consequently the scope of the usefulness of most hypnotic operators is much restricted as regard voice matters. Somewhat similarly, when the learning of pianoforte playing is the object in view, the services of an expert in that branch are desirable. The enhancing of musical memory and powers of composition and improvisation, as well as the installing of perseverance and "concentration," come well within the scope of general hypnotic treatment.

A little book, entitled *Three Aspects of Voice Production,* and long since out-of-print, evidenced that I used hypnotism as long ago as 1904 in connection with voice culture; in point of fact I commenced a few years earlier and—as I believe the Press has been correct in the assertion ofttimes made—was the first professor of voice culture to make a specialism of hypnotism in connection with his art. I was desirous, to begin with, of ascertaining whether by means of hypnotism it was practicable to eradicate diffidence and other characteristics which tended to defeat both student and teacher; and in hypnotism I found a powerful adjunct—though I early saw reason for dissenting from the then commonly-accepted theories of hypnotism. Nevertheless, until I found my way out of the maze of conflicting theories I was placed at a serious disadvantage. Being full of enthusiasm I assisted various vocalists gratuitously; but I soon found demonstrated the soundness of Sophocles' statement that "Opinion is stronger than truth." I commenced to walk more cautiously, though I continued closely to investigate and diligently to practise hypnotism. I also tested the applicability of autosuggestion as a substitute; but though I found it proved of some use, it fell far short of hypnotism in efficacy. Discretion led me to make it a stepping stone in some cases, however; and in most cases I advocated it as a supplement to hypnotism.

The artistic use of the voice, though the only physiologically correct employment of the vocal organs, like excellency in any other of the fine arts, is the result of a gradual evolution; it is not a matter that can be solved by a single individual, however richly endowed he may happen to be with common sense. Much of the early experimentation doubtless had disastrous consequences, and only by degrees was a high level of mechanical and artistic excellence reached. By the time of Handel, the main conclusions were those that formed the groundwork of the teaching of Nicolo Porpora (born 1688, at Naples), one of the greatest singing masters of his own, or any time. What is known about genuine voice culture is in all essentials consistent with Porpora's principles—even though a wider knowledge of physiology, of physics, and of psychology has enabled some of us to shorten considerably the time required to complete certain parts of training.

I remarked that much of the early vocal experimentation had doubtless disastrous consequences. Fortunately, we do not need to retrace that ground, and the attempts by uncultured vocalists to correct, or dogmatise, regarding vocal art are to be deprecated. Nevertheless, in the hands of a properly-trained vocalist, a knowledge of vocal physiology is very useful, and to the teacher of voice production it is essential to the acquirement of the best results.

About to enter its fifth large edition is a book by me on my psycho-physical method of voice culture. In that book (*Voice Culture made Easy*) I give in detail the underlying principles upon which voice culture can be safely pursued, both for speech and song, without the aid of a teacher,—and, I make bold to say, most teachers of singing are worse than useless. David Bispham, a deceased American bass singer of eminence, declared with equal humour and truth: "So many persons can sing a little and have a great longing to sing more that they will take lessons of anybody who will give them encouragement; and so incapables, casting about for a means of earning a livelihood when all else has failed, say to themselves, 'I know what I'll do; I'll teach singing!'"

The skilful voice trainer often finds good vocal material where the novice considers there is nothing but crude, unmusical noise possible. In the words of the celebrated centenarian singing master, Manuel Garcia: "It has often happened that the very qualities which judicious study has developed have been so obscured by defects at the outset that their existence has been denied altogether." "Staying at the top," Caruso once declared, "is harder than getting there." Yet, "getting there" was not the simplest task—even to him! His tutor, Vergine, was at first sceptical regarding Caruso's voice becoming sufficiently strong for professional singing, and Verdi was even more dissatisfied with it. Caruso himself was determined to succeed, though uncertain as to whether his voice was tenor or baritone. He later remarked that at that early period it resembled "the wind whistling through a window."

In dealing with the mastery of any subject, it is of

paramount importance that compounds be not mistaken for elements. If one were to judge a peal of bells by the number of changes and clangs that could be produced by means of them, the number of elements would seem innumerable. It is just the same with voice. Unless the subject be taken to pieces and the *real* elements established one by one, and gradually connected as the pupil becomes ready to connect them, the study of voice seems illimitable; consequently many persons give up, discouraged or disgusted. Nevertheless, the elements of voice culture are really very simple; and the study, when properly pursued, not only bestows upon the student a new and delightful mode of self-expression, but also a strong prophylactic against serious disease of the vital organs.

Knowing what I do of the voice, I could not be guilty of the absurdity of attempting to turn its mode of culture into blind hypnotic suggestion; I bring to bear the fundamental principles of the Old Italian School, and supplement them by many physiological, as well as by psychological, devices.

I recognise that, though voice culture is impracticable without mind power, the result of the thought brought to bear—be it good or bad—is always dependent upon the physique. I recognise, too, that mental culture and physical culture should be pursued hand-in-hand, intertwined with and supplementing each other. And, still further, I would have hypnotism adopted, not merely because it affords a condition eminently suitable for suggestive treatment, but because without it the mind of the student can rarely achieve its full efficiency.

In addition to beginners who have rapidly attained proficiency, my clientel has included many professional singers—several celebrities. The majority of these persons applied for the dissipation of nervousness or other similar handicap; but it has been far from unusual to find that they also stood in need of a physiologically sound basis for voice, and may have been passing, for several years, from teacher to teacher, spending much money in vain endeavours to overcome what should have been, at most, preliminary difficulties. Some have told me that until they came to me for assistance they had never had a genuine vocal lesson. Clearly, their teachers either knew little or nothing of the art they professed to teach, or persisted in putting the cart before the horse. Much waste of time and money would be averted if would-be singers would listen critically to their teachers' voices in order to gauge the probable ultimate effect upon themselves of the "methods" inculcated.

Recognition of misconceptions regarding hypnotism has caused many vocalists to be reticent of making public the origin of their ultimate successes, so I refrain from mentioning the names of vocalists helped hypnotically by me. But I am entitled to refer to Coué in this connection. Before we met, he was accustomed to help the vocal and musical students at the Nancy Academy; and, after he had been initiated by me in some of the underlying principles of voice production, he was able to help so effectually Mary Garden, then America's principal soprano, that she publicly stated that within one month her voice had appreciably improved and she had reached notes never sung by her before. It is one thing to please the ignorant, and a far different thing to please adepts—and Mary Garden, whatever her deficiencies, deservedly ranked very high in her profession.

In writing of my book, *Rational Hypnotism*, *Musical Opinion*, for July and September, 1914, stated editorially that it had " seldom come across a work at once so straightforward and so justly argued," and boldly taking up the theme, recommended the work and the aids advocated therein to the notice of all open-minded musicians.

In the same magazine, for February, 1924, appeared an article by me on *Psychics in Voice Culture*. " Dr. Lloyd Tuckey," I wrote, " quotes the advice of another eminent medical man to the members of his profession collectively, somewhat as follows : ' Gentlemen, do not let us be hypnotists instead of doctors, but *let us be prepared to employ* hypnotism where it is likely to be serviceable.' Braid, though he widely employed so-called ' hypnotism ' with patients, objected to being called a ' hypnotist,' protesting that he was no more a hypnotist than a ' castor oil ' doctor. Surely, members of other professions may well take a hint from the medical men referred to! It is not derogatory to a musician or other art specialist to be skilled in methodical suggestion. On the contrary, the possession of that skill is rather an evidence that the specialist is resolved to keep abreast of the times, and it should tend to convince the general public that a like zeal will be manifested throughout his work—that thoroughness and efficiency are keynotes of his character. Moreover, when the great personal intellectual advantages accruing from a knowledge of psychics be taken into account, it becomes obvious that, far from being a diversion from the straight path to professional excellence, the additional knowledge, absorbed and utilised, will have made him better able to utilize all other knowledge of which he is possessed, and have even materially aided in the increase of his knowledge and powers."

A properly-produced voice is the essential basis upon which the superstructure of vocal eloquence can be erected. Without that basis, all attempts at vocal expression are more or less caricatures. It is far from enough to have clear pronunciation; the singing of the words should enhance their import, whereas it usually detracts from or disguises it. There is, in good singing, a sort of analogy to speech, and that analogy is present wherever song differs in kind from speech; and I hope to place before the public, in the not far-distant future, a work, on *Eloquence in Speech and Song,* which will be based on sound psychological principles and will, I believe, be well calculated to help aspiring vocalists to deserve that for which they yearn.

CHAPTER XVIII

THE PLATFORM, THE PULPIT & THE STAGE

THE celebrated Lord Chesterfield remarked that orators and comets are usually looked upon with an equal degree of wonder, and added that in reality considerable eloquence is acquirable by almost anyone. Surely there is no insuperable obstacle preventing the ordinary person from delivering with force and some grace the ideas that automatically arise into consciousness. Unfortunately, although there is a wholesome conviction in the mind of nearly everyone that close application is necessary to whoever would make a pronounced success of public singing, special preparation of a somewhat similar and overlapping character is rarely considered of more than trifling, if of any, importance to efficient speaking. There can be no greater mistake, however. The ancient Greeks and Romans knew better; with them the art of speaking was held to be a branch of education essential to every student and to health. Looked at from the hygienic standpoint, is it not a significant fact that, as shown by statistics, at least three-fifths of London school teachers suffer from chronic laryngitis, a direct result of voice abuse? Observations of others besides myself point to the conclusion that an even larger proportion of clergymen suffer from follicular sore throat (*disphonia clericorum*).

To public speaker and public singer alike power of voice is of paramount importance, and if the knowledge of how to get it in a legitimate manner be absent, another way is tried, and frequently with disastrous results. This is another of the instances where, however, putting the horse before the cart can in general rectify matters speedily.

Numerous singers, clergymen, lawyers, actors, auctioneers and others have applied to me for assistance. In a large proportion of these cases definite vocal instruction was indicated as advisable, and in a considerable number of instances, was indispensable. To attempt to deal with such cases by hypnotism solely is sheer quackery; indeed, it would hardly be just to ascribe to the sufferers a deficiency in self-confidence, for had they been self-confident they would also have been swollen-headed. With most of these persons a rightly-placed self-confidence would naturally tend to grow alongside control and development of voice. That was not the whole matter, however. Public speaking demands some histrionic ability and the power of thinking steadily when face to face with an audience—perhaps of a critical nature. Those are directions in which hypnotism can prove a friend indeed. It should ever be remembered that to possess feeling and imagination, and to be able rightly and vividly to express emotions and awaken them in others are by no means identical.

Among clergymen who have been treated by me hypnotically, I have had but one failure. The exception was due to the client's inebriety being carefully concealed from me. Whoever solicits the aid of an hypnotic operator should have so chosen as to be able to confide in him completely, any lack of candour is liable to interpose an obstacle to successful treatment. The other clergymen became fluent speakers, able and accustomed to relying almost entirely upon brain work unconscious to them as individuals to work out their discourses on general lines decided upon.

A quotation from my broadcast from Atlantic City on 18th August 1937 may be worth quoting. " The circumstance is deplorable," I remarked, " that sensationalism, not the dissemination of truth, is, or seems to be, the main, if not the sole, object of all the films yet seen by me that introduce ' hypnotism '—and my home is at the centre of the British film industry, . . . where my aid as an hypnotic practitioner is sought by film actors and actresses who themselves are free from any illusions as to the mental condition I induce and utilise." A well-known film director had brought to me an actress for treatment, and was sufficiently interested in the results achieved that he himself visited me for help and instruction; but he assured me that the bulk of persons habituated to attending cinemas wanted to be amused, not instructed—a statement which seemed to be borne out by his later activities in relation to film-" hypnotism ". Films such as *The Seventh Veil* are very misleading. Neither sodium pentathol nor any other drug induces hypnosis.

The general public little suspects how often those of us who are seriously interested in the advancement and proper application of hypnotism are appealed to by theatrical people to give them secretly the impetus which they have long needed to enable them to make their mark. Many actors and actresses who have risen to the heights of histrionic fame would never have obtained that eminence but for the help afforded by hypnotism skilfully applied. To those who are sufficiently enamoured with the stage to have made ungrudgingly the sacrifices it demands of its votaries and yet feel that there is something in themselves "holding them back," I would say, very earnestly: "Try what hypnotism can do for you. You are extremely unlikely to be disappointed with the result of the test."

CHAPTER XIX

SPEECH DEFECTS

THIS is a subject so wide that to deal with it thoroughly requires very much more space than can be given to it in this volume. For further details I beg to refer to my book, *The Cure of Stammering, Stuttering and Other Functional Speech Disorders.*

Some cases of speech defect are results of malformation, disease, or injury, either of the vocal organs or of the brain centre especially associated therewith—situated in the left half of the brain in right-handed people, and in the right half in left-handed. Cases of cleft palate and extreme instances of short tongue or of tongue-tie, are included in this category; but there are many cases that are supposed to belong to it which, in reality, are the outcome of suggestion and ignorance combined. For example, a person slightly tongue-tied may be allowed and expected to speak badly, and nevertheless may be potentially capable of speaking well. Few children operated upon for the removal of the tongue-tied condition really need the operation.

Some gravely organic cases of speech defect are incurable. Sometimes a skilful surgeon may effect a cure; and in some other cases appliances are of much service.

Functional cases include mutism—which is inability to even whisper—aphonia, which is loss of ability to speak otherwise than in a whisper; and stammering, stuttering, tremulousness, and hesitating speech. All such cases should be looked upon as curable; they proceed from imitation, or diffidence, or emotional shock, or attempted repression of distasteful ideas and feelings, or suggestion combined with one or more of those causes.

The terms "stammering" and "stuttering," though often used interchangeably, should be clearly differentiated. If a person when trying to say "two" cannot do more for a time than press his lips together, he is stammering; if, on the other hand, he says "t-t-t-t-two," he is stuttering. "Stammering," as wrote Charles Lunn, "is a stoppage that cannot be moved; stuttering is a movement that cannot be stopped." The defects referred to may exist in the same individual, though, as a rule, stammerers are inclined to be excitable and vivacious; stutterers shy and reserved. In many cases the predispositions are inherited, and debility is sufficient to give rise to the speech complaint. But for the fact that during the debility the defects tend to become firmly rooted habits, one might reasonably conclude that, as happens in some cases, the speech would by degrees become normal alongside restoration to health. However, the effect of involuntary suggestion should always be taken into account; for, though suggestion is not the only cause of stammering or stuttering, probably it is always concerned with the continuance of the trouble. An alteration in mental attitude and outlook is an important part in the competent treatment of stammerers and stutterers—just as of other sufferers.

For many years I have had a very wide experience, war hospital as well as other, in the treatment of functional speech defects; and although I allow the value in many—I might almost say "most"—cases of physiological aids, the truth has been continually forced under my notice that, in the vast majority of cases, psychological treatment is essential to cure—even when physiological devices are of service to no mean extent. Most of the patients who came under my care in war hospitals were neurasthenics and, by keeping nerves and muscles on tension, they wasted much energy and continually thwarted themselves in their endeavours, physical and mental. The strictly vocal therapeutic part of their treatment could not fail to be of service; but it was mainly due to my practical knowledge of psychology being combined with my skill in voice culture that enabled me to bring about results described by the journalists (invited by educational officers to attend classes) as "wonderful," "astounding."

In my experience many sufferers, of every kind of functional speech defect, have immediately proved amenable to treatment. Such cases apply particularly to youth. However, many ex-soldiers who stammered or stuttered in consequence of experiences during the World Wars were cured very rapidly. That was rarely the case with ex-soldiers who had previously defective speech made worse by the war. Certain of the men were evidently passed for service through their defect showing itself only intermittently. One individual who volunteered for service fancied that he had been accepted, but no—

"The doctor won't pass you," explained the sergeant; "You are marked 'Medically unfit'—he says you stammer."

The would-be soldier was indignant: "Stammering isn't being medically unfit," he protested.

"Perhaps not," commented the sergeant; "But if your company were stationed in the park, and when you were walking out you didn't answer the sentry's challenge, you *very soon would be* medically unfit!"

When I first came into contact with Coué he believed and publicly stated that persons stammered and stuttered through expectation solely, that what occurred in the first instance through nervous excitement was continued through auto-suggestion.

I asked him: "If a person stammered or stuttered on one occasion through nervous excitement, what is there to prevent him from doing so again?" Coué recognised immediately that he had overlooked points, and at a later date jointly stated with me: "There are cases in which other agents in addition to it" ("auto-suggestion") "are not merely advisable, but indispensable."

Many cases of speech defect connected with the World Wars were due to attempted suppression of memories and connected emotions. The persistence of the recollection led to hesitation, and sometimes to stammering, stuttering, or even worse. The symptoms were the result of a kind of panic which (figuratively) fed upon the troubles it created; in other words, auto-suggestion was largely responsible for the dire effects. As the trouble progressed the sufferers became definitely psychasthenic.

Hypnotism, when used to cure speech defects, should be looked upon as not wholly a suggestive agent, but, and in many cases more particularly, as a means of " tapping " the mental reservoir and thus bringing into the full light of conscious knowledge whatever ideas, partially or completely submerged, lie at the root of the trouble. I readily admit that with children, and some adults, such probing is not indispensable; nevertheless, in nearly every case it is a reasonable precaution against relapse. Further, if the speech defect should happen to be merely the symptom of an undiscovered cause, by ignoring that cause one runs the risk of merely exchanging symptoms. Time, energy and money are often spent in profusion on useless—and worse than useless—endeavours to be cured of speech disorders that, though seemingly severe, may nevertheless admit of ready cure by a genuine expert.

CHAPTER XX

HYPNOTISM FROM NEW VIEWPOINTS (AVIATION, RADIO, TELEVISION, ETC.)

INDIVIDUAL and confidential contact between client and operator is indispensable for the successful hypnotic treatment of certain types of cases. Moreover, as an expert operator is able to learn many things by visual observation of clients and can thus make his treatment more exactly fit the requirements of a case, his presence is sometimes advisable though perhaps not essential. On the other hand there are numerous cases that can be treated otherwise. Since the beginning of the present century I have sometimes employed hypnotism by telephone, and in 1925 I advocated gramophonic hypnotism; but I have gone still further.

The *Sunday Graphic* of 11th November, 1934, contained the following news-item:—

"I have just witnessed an experiment in which a man of 65 was hypnotised over the telephone and then taken for an aeroplane ride. Seated in a telephone box at Hanworth Aerodrome, with Rita, his daughter, holding the receiver to his ear, Mr. Joseph Hyde was hypnotised by Mr. Louis Orton from his home at Uxbridge. Mr. Hyde was in a state of hypnosis at the telephone for five minutes. Then, accompanied by his daughter, he walked to the aeroplane while curious pilots and mechanics stood around. The aeroplane flew at a height of 2,000 feet for a quarter of an hour, and on landing I interviewed Mr. Hyde. 'Hypnotism applied by Mr. Orton cured me of complete blindness in the right eye eighteen months ago,' he told me. 'What happened in the telephone box is practically a blank to me. I was suddenly awakened to the fact that dense clouds were around me and that I was flying at 2,000 feet. I was also surprised to see a man behind me taking photographs; he had de-hypnotised me in the air through the medium of Mr. Orton's suggestions.' Mr. Hyde told me that it was the first time he had ever flown, and that he would never have done so without first being hypnotised. 'The flight was lovely —all my fears were dispelled,' he said. Mr. Orton told me on the telephone that he had been hypnotising people 'over the wire' for thirty-four years."

The Dublin Evening Herald and other newspapers remarked on my use of the 'phone "to keep in touch with patients in different parts of the country." That was correct; but the statement: "Mr. Orton finds it easier in some cases to psycho-analyse a person by 'phone than by personal interview" was due to misapprehension. As an auxiliary to hypnotism in person, telephonic hypnotism can be of incalculable value sometimes; but, in general, telephonic hypnotism must take a subordinate place to hypnotism in person.

Another experiment was thus reported, amusingly, in *The Star*: "Mr. Harold Follis, of Firs Avenue,

Muswell Hill, has been sent to sleep by wireless. So have lots of other people, but this is different. Mr. J. Louis Orton, of Uxbridge, sent Mr. Follis out in a motor-car around Grays, with an observer and a three-valve wireless receiver. Mr. Follis donned the head-phones and heard Mr. Orton hypnotising him into sleep. The car was three miles out of Grays when Mr. Follis went to sleep. 'I remember Mr. Orton's first suggestions, "drowsiness" and "sleep," then things became hazy,' he said."

Another experiment was in effect an extension of that described in my chapter on Mental and Nervous Complaints. *Popular Wireless* stated: "The idea of hypnotising people to give them air confidence—to which I referred recently—has now been tried out with marked success. The subject was Mrs. Ian Coward, who had feared heights all her life. Her husband, who is an ardent airman, could never persuade her to try a flight, but after hypnotic suggestion from Mr. J. Louis Orton, she went for a forty-mile flip in a stiff breeze. You may have heard G2YH transmitting to the 'plane when it was over Grays. But nothing heard then was so surprising to her friends as the fact that when Mrs. Coward alighted, she was still unperturbed and calmly inquired: 'What about lunch?'"

My next medium for hypnotic procedure was television. The following quotation is from *The People* for 3rd February, 1935:—

"A sixteen-year-old girl was hypnotised by television at the Uxbridge home of Mr. Louis Orton, the hypnotist, to-day.

"Rita Hyde, who is being treated for eye trouble, was seated in a chair 'looking-in' at a television receiver, through a mirror suspended above her head. Close by was a loud speaker.

"As pictures of the hypnotist making passes with his hands were thrown on to the mirror, a voice was heard:

"'You feel drowsy. Your arms and legs feel heavy. You are falling fast asleep. Sleep.'

"The hypnotist's eyes appeared to look right through the television receiver. The girl suddenly lapsed into a deep hypnosis.

"When she awakened she said to me: 'I feel very well and happy, but I remember nothing excepting the first few words Mr. Orton spoke.' . . .

"Mr. Orton told me that the pictures were reflected from the mirror to allow his subject to recline in a chair. 'Lying back at ease is conducive to good hypnotism,' he said."

Later, I successfully attempted hypnotism by cinema-talkie. That experiment formed part of what were laboratory experiments concerned with the problem of road-safety, a subject which will be dealt with in my next chapter.

CHAPTER XXI

HYPNOTISM AND ROAD SAFETY

By the hypnotic experiments detailed in my twentieth chapter I had endeavoured to clear the ground somewhat for a proposal which I put before our Ministry of Transport. I deemed some persons would consider the proposal fantastic—perhaps insane; others would consider it as satanic, and some might even think they scented in it a deeply-laid—not to say "nefarious"—scheme to become dictator. But my hypnotic experiments in connection with aviation, the telephone, radio and television, were reported in the national, provincial, technical and, indeed, international press, and certainly led millions of persons to look—transiently, if no more—at hypnotism in lights that were to them novel.

My proposal was instituted in order to bring about, if possible, in a gigantic way what I had hitherto done with a comparative few. A decade, indeed, had elapsed since I tested the efficacy of hypnotism in relation to motor driving, and my attempts had invariably met with mutually gratifying results.

Mr. Hore-Belisha, when Minister of Transport, pointed out publicly that all traffic signals and other mechanical expedients, devised or devisable, were necessarily incomplete safeguards, *the real safety device being the spirit of unremitting care and attention.* I venture to add that mental factors may obscure, or even conceal, whatever merit the mechanical factors may possess in themselves. Still further: it may even happen that the mechanical and mental factors may each oppose the other—as I shall attempt to show.

Persons may be careless, and persons may be incapable of acting aright in emergencies. Memory, observation, decision, and favourable association of physical as well as of mental activities, need to be taken adequately into account.

Penalties, though necessary up to a point, can tend to cause temporarily paralysing nervousness. Pleading may help, but it can also lead to paralysing fear. To entreat persons to "take extra care" can lead to bungling on their part. Moreover, the drunkard's self-defeat through lack of self-confidence is typical of many persons' behaviour under stress.

My hypnotic experiments with individuals abolished fear of driving at all, awkwardness in driving, and eye-strain. What I had done for the few, I proposed to do for the many. I considered that the only valid objections that could be raised to my scheme would be products of ignorance or misapprehension.

Adequate preparation of the general public would be essential to the success of the scheme; curiosity, a wholesome interest, and, as far as practicable, enthusiasm would need to be evoked and enhanced. The truth would need to be driven home that the results of the verbal suggestions, which I proposed to give to the mass by radio, would be dependent upon my hearers' ability, essentially, to actualise them, and that inasmuch as non-compliance can, and sometimes does, proceed from caprice, *willing compliance* obviously would play a part in the induction of the later phenomena as well as in the induction of the prime condition—hypnosis. I should need to assist skilfully in the induction of hypnosis, and in correctly arranging and presenting the ideas which, when accepted, absorbed, and utilised, would become, in effect, part of each hearer's personality, which would thus be enriched.

The methodical suggestion for these purposes should, I consider, take place for the first time a few days later than a preparatory speech. Prefacing the practical side, a short resumé of the earlier speech might well be given. That would be followed by a few experiments calculated to instil confidence regarding the safety and efficacy of the main procedure about to be carried out. These preliminary experiments would relate to mental tension, mental relaxation, reversed effort (or the misdirection of energy through doubt), and so on. The suggestions relating to road traffic would be led up to by means of a non-mystical routine. In establishing the capability of entering a contemplative mood readily and at will, I should guard, by special verbal suggestion, against the abuse of that capability—which abuse could, at times, be a possible source of danger to drivers and to pedestrians.

Each performance of the mass-suggestion broadcast might last half-an-hour. Periodical repetition of the broadcast, but not of the original speech—unless desired, would be essential to getting the best results. Children being readily helped by hypnotism, broadcasts to schools could advantageously be carried out.

As cramping and partial immobility of the mental powers can, by means of hypnotic suggestion, be practically abolished, and the capacity of easy, prompt, rapid and comprehensive thought can be established, radio mass-hypnotism, if carried out in the way I advocate, would, by changing mental outlook and attitude, enhance the intellectual, and therefore the material, well-being of the nation or nations concerned.

The *Evening Standard* of the 26th January, 1935, stated:—

> "Mr. Hore-Belisha, the Minister of Transport, is considering a plan to hypnotise people over the radio so as to make them 'traffic conscious.'
>
> "Mr. J. Louis Orton, who claims that within 35 years he has hypnotised 30,000 people, has offered to undertake from the B.B.C. a radio experiment in mass-suggestion. The idea is that listeners would automatically carry out the suggestions made by Mr. Orton, and thus the number of street accidents would be reduced.
>
> "The *Evening Standard* was told at the Ministry of Transport that the suggestion will receive full consideration from the Minister.
>
> "'We ourselves have no evidence that people can be hypnotised by wireless,' an official stated, 'but the Minister is prepared to investigate every aspect of the traffic problem.'

". . . In an interview with the *Evening Standard* to-day, Mr. Orton . . . outlined his plans. '. . . I should require the full co-operation of listeners. My idea is to use hypnotic suggestion over the radio for the purpose of enabling a person to do the right thing in an emergency. I should begin by requiring listeners' whole attention. Having got this, I should proceed with my usual routine for causing a brown study. . . . This may sound outlandish, but I am convinced it can be done if listeners will co-operate.'"

My first experiment in radio mass-hypnotism for road safety was carried out (unofficially) from G—5XK, a private transmitting station, working on 40 metres, at Huddersfield. It was undertaken solely as a test of mass radio-hypnotism. "Unfortunately," stated the *News Chronicle* of 7th Februarv. 1935. "the atmospherics decided to take a hand in the game, and all we heard for half-an-hour or so were blasts, roars, the local electricity station and the Lockwood nightingale." Had the correspondent concerned waited a little longer, he would have been better prepared to form a just decision. Almost without exception the press was well disposed and reported accordingly. Nevertheless, I regret to have to add that the atmospheric conditions proved a serious, though not an insuperable, obstacle.

Mr. Hore-Belisha expressed his "appreciation of the trouble" I had "taken to bring before him this new method of approach to the serious problem of road safety." The difficulty, I was informed, partly lay with matters outside the Ministry; but it was suggested that I should strengthen my position in the matter by undertaking a control experiment—after the example of Pasteur. This proposal was that I should test the efficacy of mass radio-hypnotism in some other direction than road safety, the contention of the Ministry being that the numerous and variable factors at work made impracticable any attempt to decide as to the efficacy of any single factor. I appreciated that, from the standpoint of the Ministry (though not from my own standpoint), the test was advisable as a precaution, so I gladly undertook to comply with the proposal made. After an unavoidable delay the experimentation was carried out in a hall at Denham, Bucks.

The experiment was a double one. The mass hypnotism was by radio, and, so far as I am aware, none of the special persons, volunteers from the audience, had been previously hypnotised. The first set of suggestions was applied to the improvement of sight, as being something which could be readily tested both before and after the radio mass-hypnotism, and is an actual factor *unquestionably affecting road safety.*

Perhaps I should remark here that practically every untrained person suffers, to a degree hardly credible to the uninitiated, from asthenopia, which is warped sight not due to alteration in the shape or texture of the eye. Asthenopia is a result of incorrect employment of the optical apparatus, and is functional, not organic, in character; thus, the trouble being almost universal, whether the eyes are so shaped as to signify short, or medium, or long sight, a definite increase in range and clarity of vision can be induced by hypnotic procedures.

The second set of suggestions, given without interval after those relating to sight, were definitely directed to road safety. They were addressed to pedestrians as well as to motorists.

Of the six volunteers, the sight of five proved to be markedly better after the mass radio-hypnotism. The exception was a man, sixty-three years of age, who claimed to have been unaffected by any part of the hypnotic procedure. (I learn that he has died since from Addison's disease.) The tests before and after the experiment were checked by an outsider. Two journalists who were present were rather sceptical, and volunteered for a test of hypnotism in relation to their own sight; and after I had complied with the proposal, both sportingly admitted their defeat. One of these journalists represented the *Middlesex Advertiser,* in which paper he recorded his astonishment that his sight had become a foot longer for the reading of small print.

The mass radio-hypnotism was shown to be capable of inducing *profound* hypnosis despite previous unacquaintance with the condition, and also despite hard chairs and an inquisitive audience.

Inasmuch as the suggestions applied to sight were successful, there is surely good reason for concluding that the suggestions applied to road safety were so too. The Ministry, however, raised another question, *viz.,* that persons who had come into contact with me were not in the position of complete strangers; what was wanted was that the experiments should be conducted through a big broadcasting station, so that persons anywhere and almost everywhere would be the recipients of my suggestions.

Gathering that my proposals, to be accepted by the British Broadcasting Corporation, would need to be recommended by the Ministry of Transport, I felt that the wisest course would be to take, when opportunities occurred, other means to further the end in view.

When touring the United States during 1937, I returned to the attack. Timidity, or something which, to my eyes, resembled it, affected certain sections of the press; but I found no difficulty as regards the broadcasting stations—including some of the foremost in the whole world. My broadcasts being on short waves as well as long, my views were given worldwide publicity. The U.S.A. station officials were enthusiastic regarding my broadcasts, arrangements were made for continuance of the propaganda, and only the nearness of the day when I was due back in England prevented me from carrying out the whole of the experiments as described in this chapter. Regretfully I could not see my way to comply with a proposal, sent from Oklahoma in December 1951, that I should again visit the U.S.A. "and accept engagements to demonstrate this phenomenon for various oil companies, etc." Just possibly a favourable time will come. The cause is dear to my heart, and, had the Indian radio officials been allowed by the government, my successful broadcasts from Bombay and New Delhi (in 1949) would have been followed by radio mass-hypnotism to promote road safety and, further, for bringing about all-round mental and physical improvement and progress. I was informed that the Indian government was fearful of sanctioning what, it might be thought (though erroneously), was prompted by political and party motives, and therefore likely to have severe repercussions on the sponsors. Alas! the day when my ardent wishes as regards road-safety may long be retarded, but will assuredly come. There are clear signs that a small section of the medical profession is seizing the opportunity presented, and I am pleased to observe even that belated interest. It rests with practitioners who recognise the real nature of hypnotism to do their best to assist the few who need help and maybe have the vision to seek it.

In this connection I am reminded of the invention, by Mrs. Hertha Ayrton, of a fan to clear away deadly gases during the War of 1914-1918. She offered the scheme and the invention to the nation, and free of all charges, but a year elapsed before the invention was tried in the trenches. Five-thousand fans were then ordered, but not until thousands more of brave men had been unnecessary victims of gassing.

When will officialdom pay due heed to what I contend is a tried and effectual measure for reducing the enormous toll of the roads?

CHAPTER XXII

FUNDAMENTAL CONCLUSIONS

THE following facts should be universally known:—

(1) Hypnosis is not, in the true sense, an artificial condition, though induced by deft contrivances; it is a condition characteristic of a supposedly favoured few, but can be made a characteristic of practically everybody as required for serviceable purposes.

(2) The person operated upon is not rendered, even temporarily, more credulous or obedient. The condition induced is absolutely harmless. The operator is at most merely an efficient helper—and an inefficient operator may be a hinderer or even a preventer. The condition can later be obtained and used by the erstwhile " subject."

(3) If it were needful for you to get to a distant place as speedily as possible, you would not be disposed to walk rather than make use of a convenient and available vehicle. Hypnotic procedures correspond to that vehicle; they are commonly the quickest and best aids to achievement, for they get at its very basis. Frequently, hypnotism enables persons to get where they otherwise never would, or could.

(4) " Physical " treatment by means of hypnotism is really physical culture of an advanced character, consequently should be used as a preventive as well as a remedy. The power which one possesses potentially over one's own organism is colossal. Thought of a morbid nature may kill, and its reverse may bring about marvellous cures.

(5) Hypnotism is a part of mental hygiene, and therefore should be used as a part of ordinary education—physical, intellectual and moral. It is the best aid in existence for the uprooting of harmful habits, and for the implanting and cultivation of good habits.

(6) Prevention being better than cure, every child should have the advantages that hypnotism offers. Behind seeming incapacity often lies marked capacity—capacity sometimes revealed eventually by hypnotic procedure.

In this connection may I remind you of two lines from Shakespeare? They run:—

> " Cease to lament for that thou canst not help,
> And study help for that which thou lament'st."

GLOSSARY

Contemplative Mood.—A temporary mental state, tending towards contemplation—internal or external.

Ecstatics.—Persons carried away, by excessive emotion, beyond normal sensibility.

Empiricism.—Relying on experience.

Functional Complaints.—Complaints that do not involve a definite change of structure. See Organic Complaints.

Hypnosis.—The mental condition (not morbid) of a hypnotised person. An artificially-induced contemplative mood.

Hypnotee.—A hypnotised person or " subject." See Subject.

Hypnotism.—From a Greek word meaning "sleep"; but really, hypnotism is the art and science concerned with the systematic (as contrasted with the haphazard) training, development, and utilisation of Attention.

Hysteria.—A nervous affection of functional nature. See Functional Complaints.

Idiosyncrasy.—Individual peculiarity—physical or mental.

Intention.—Contemplation.

Mesmerism.—In practice almost synonymous with "hypnotism," but theoretically in accordance with the notions of F. A. Mesmer.

Organic Complaints.—Complaints which involve a definite change of structure. See Functional Complaints.

Objectively.—As something external to oneself.

Observative Mood.—The opposite of "absence of mind." See Contemplative Mood.

Oracle.—Among the ancient Greeks and Romans, words supposed to be delivered by the gods—often through persons in a condition of "trance." See Trance.

Phenomenon.—In the scientific sense, something that can be observed, not necessarily particularly wonderful.

Somnambule.—A sleep-walker, or a person in an alert condition of hypnosis—formerly supposed to be sleep.

Somnambulism.—Literally "sleep-walking." The term is also applied to an alert condition of hypnosis.

Stimulus.—Something which arouses action.

Subject.—As used by me simply denotes the subject of an experiment, and does not infer that the person is dominated partially even.

Subjectively.—In the light of introspection. The opposite of "objectively."

Suggestibility.—Proneness to accept as true, and to act in accordance with, suggestions made.

Suggestion.—Psychologically, a *suggestion* is an *idea.* (To *suggest* is to express an idea—in words or otherwise.) "Suggestion" is also applied to the art and science of impressing ideas on oneself or others.

Trance.—Means a "passing," and originally referred to the notion that when a person was entranced his or her "soul" passed from the body. Sometimes means "an ecstacy."

Volition.—The *will*, or the act of willing, or choosing, or resolving.

WILSHIRE Self-Improvement LIBRARY

_____ABILITY TO LOVE *by Dr. Allan Fromme*	$2.00
_____ACT YOUR WAY TO SUCCESSFUL LIVING *Neil & Margaret Rau*	2.00
_____ADVANCED TECHNIQUES OF HYPNOSIS *Melvin Powers*	1.00
_____ANIMAL HYPNOSIS *Dr. F. A. Völgyesi*	2.00
_____ASTROLOGY FOR EVERYDAY LIVING *Janet Harris*	2.00
_____ASTROLOGY GUIDE TO GOOD HEALTH *Alexandra Kayhle*	2.00
_____ASTROLOGY MADE EASY *by Astarte*	2.00
_____ASTROLOGY MADE PRACTICAL *Alexandra Kayhle*	2.00
_____CHESS MADE EASY *Milton L. Hanauer*	1.00
_____CHESS PROBLEMS FOR BEGINNERS *edited by Fred Reinfeld*	1.00
_____CHESS TACTICS FOR BEGINNERS *edited by Fred Reinfeld*	1.00
_____CHILDBIRTH WITH HYPNOSIS *William S. Kroger, M.D.*	2.00
_____CONCENTRATION–A Guide to Mental Mastery *Mouni Sadhu*	2.00
_____CONVERSATION MADE EASY *Elliot Russell*	1.00
_____CYBERNETICS WITHIN US *Y. Saparina*	2.00
_____DOCTOR PYGMALION *Maxwell Maltz, M.D.*	2.00
_____DREAMS & OMENS REVEALED *Fred Gettings*	2.00
_____DR. LINDNER'S SPECIAL WEIGHT CONTROL METHOD *P. Lindner*	1.00
_____DYNAMIC THINKING *Melvin Powers*	1.00
_____EAT, THINK & BE SLENDER *Leonid Kotkin, M.D.*	2.00
_____ENCYCLOPEDIA OF MODERN SEX & LOVE TECHNIQUES *by R. Macandrew*	2.00
_____EXAM SECRET *Dennis B. Jackson*	1.00
_____15 MASTER KEYS TO SUCCESS, POPULARITY & PRESTIGE *C. W. Bailey*	2.00
_____FORTUNE TELLING WITH CARDS *P. Foli*	2.00
_____GROW RICH WHILE YOU SLEEP *Ben Sweetland*	2.00
_____GUIDE TO HAPPINESS *Dr. Maxwell S. Cagan*	2.00
_____GUIDE TO RATIONAL LIVING *Albert Ellis, Ph.D. & R. Harper, Ph.D.*	2.00
_____GUIDE TO SUCCESSFUL LIVING *Joe D. Batten & Leonard C. Hudson*	2.00
_____GUIDE TO SUCCESSFUL MARRIAGE *Drs. Albert Ellis & R. Harper*	2.00
_____HANDWRITING ANALYSIS MADE EASY *John Marley*	2.00
_____HARMONICA PLAYING FOR FUN & PROFIT *Hal Leighton*	3.00
_____HEALING POWER OF HERBS *May Bethel*	2.00
_____HELP YOURSELF TO BETTER SIGHT *Margaret Darst Corbett*	2.00
_____HELPING YOURSELF WITH PSYCHIATRY *Frank S. Caprio, M.D.*	2.00
_____HERBS FOR HEALTH How To Grow & Use Them *Louise Evans Doole*	2.00
_____HOW TO ATTRACT GOOD LUCK *A. H. Z. Carr*	2.00
_____HOW TO DEVELOP A BETTER SPEAKING VOICE *M. Hellier*	1.00
_____HOW TO DEVELOP AN EXCEPTIONAL MEMORY *Young and Gibson*	2.00
_____HOW TO IMPROVE YOUR BRIDGE *Alfred Sheinwold*	2.00
_____HOW TO LIVE A RICHER & FULLER LIFE *Rabbi Edgar F. Magnin*	2.00
_____HOW TO MAKE MONEY IN REAL ESTATE *Stanley L. McMichael*	2.00

_____HOW TO OVERCOME YOUR FEARS *M. P. Leahy, M.D.* 2.00
_____HOW TO SLEEP WITHOUT PILLS *Dr. David F. Tracy* 1.00
_____HOW TO SOLVE YOUR SEX PROBLEMS
WITH SELF-HYPNOSIS *F. Caprio, M.D.* 2.00
_____HOW TO STOP SMOKING THRU SELF-HYPNOSIS *Leslie M. LeCron* 2.00
_____HOW TO UNDERSTAND YOUR DREAMS *Geoffrey A. Dudley* 2.00
_____HOW TO USE AUTO-SUGGESTION EFFECTIVELY *John Duckworth* 2.00
_____HOW TO WIN AT BRIDGE *by Edwin Kantar* 2.00
_____HOW TO WIN AT CHECKERS *Fred Reinfeld* 2.00
_____HOW TO WIN AT POKER *Terence Reese & Anthony T. Watkins* 1.00
_____HOW YOU CAN BOWL BETTER USING SELF-HYPNOSIS *Jack Heise* 2.00
_____HOW YOU CAN HAVE CONFIDENCE AND POWER *Les Giblin* 2.00
_____HOW YOU CAN PLAY BETTER GOLF USING SELF-HYPNOSIS *Heise* 2.00
_____HOW YOU CAN STOP SMOKING PERMANENTLY *Ernest Caldwell* 1.00
_____HYPNOSIS AND SELF-HYPNOSIS *Bernard Hollander, M.D.* 2.00
_____HYPNOTISM *Carl Sextus* 2.00
_____HYPNOTISM & ESP *Simeon Edmunds* 2.00
_____HYPNOTISM MADE PRACTICAL *Louis Orton* 2.00
_____HYPNOTISM REVEALED *Melvin Powers* 1.00
_____HYPNOTISM TODAY *Leslie LeCron & Jean Bordeaux, Ph.D.* 2.00
_____HYPNOTIST'S CASE BOOK *Alex Erskine* 1.00
_____I WILL *Ben Sweetland* 2.00
_____INCREASE YOUR LEARNING POWER *Geoffrey A. Dudley* 1.00
_____JUGGLING MADE EASY *Rudolf Dittrich* 1.00
_____LEFT-HANDED PEOPLE *Michael Barsley* 2.00
_____LSD–THE AGE OF MIND *Bernard Roseman* 2.00
_____MAGIC IN YOUR MIND *U. S. Andersen* 2.00
_____MAGIC OF THINKING BIG *Dr. David J. Schwartz* 2.00
_____MAGIC POWER OF YOUR MIND *Walter M. Germain* 2.00
_____MEDICAL HYPNOSIS HANDBOOK *Drs. Van Pelt, Ambrose, Newbold* 2.00
_____MENTAL POWER THRU SLEEP SUGGESTION *Melvin Powers* 1.00
_____MENTAL TELEPATHY EXPLAINED *Hereward Carrington* .50
_____MIND OVER PLATTER *Peter G. Lindner, M.D.* 2.00
_____MODERN HYPNOSIS *Lesley Kuhn & Salvatore Russo, Ph.D.* 2.00
_____MODERN NUMEROLOGY *Morris C. Goodman* 2.00
_____MY WORLD OF ASTROLOGY *Sydney Omarr* 2.00
_____NATURE'S MEDICINES *Richard Lucas* 2.00
_____NEW CARBOHYDRATE DIET COUNTER *Patti Lopez-Pereira* 1.00
_____NEW CONCEPTS OF HYPNOSIS *Bernard C. Gindes, M.D.* 2.00
_____NEW GUIDE TO INTELLIGENT REDUCING *Gayelord Hauser* 2.00
_____NUMEROLOGY–ITS FACTS AND SECRETS *by Ariel Yvon Taylor* 2.00
_____1001 BRILLIANT WAYS TO CHECKMATE *Fred Reinfeld* 2.00
_____1001 WINNING CHESS SACRIFICES & COMBINATIONS *Fred Reinfeld* 2.00
_____ORIENTAL SECRETS OF GRACEFUL LIVING *Boye De Mente* 1.00
_____OUR JEWISH HERITAGE *Rabbi Alfred Wolf & Joseph Gaer* 2.00
_____PALMISTRY MADE EASY *Fred Gettings* 2.00
_____PALMISTRY MADE PRACTICAL *Elizabeth Daniels Squire* 2.00
_____PALMISTRY SECRETS REVEALED *Henry Frith* 2.00
_____PEYOTE STORY *Bernard Roseman* 1.00
_____PRACTICAL GUIDE TO BETTER CONCENTRATION *Melvin Powers* 2.00
_____PRACTICAL GUIDE TO SELF-HYPNOSIS *Melvin Powers* 2.00
_____PRACTICAL HYPNOTISM *Philip Magonet, M.D.* 1.00
_____PRACTICAL YOGA *Ernest Wood* 2.00
_____PRACTICE OF HYPNOTIC SUGGESTION *George C. Kingsbury, M.D.* 1.00

____PSYCHEDELIC ECSTASY *William Marshall & Gilbert W. Taylor* 2.00
____PSYCHO-CYBERNETICS *Maxwell Maltz, M.D.* 2.00
____PSYCHOLOGY OF HANDWRITING *Nadya Olyanova* 2.00
____PSYCHOSOMATIC GYNECOLOGY *William S. Kroger, M.D.* 10.00
____SCIENTIFIC HYPNOTISM *Ralph Winn, Ph.D.* 1.00
____SECRET OF BOWLING STRIKES *Dawson Taylor* 2.00
____SECRET OF PERFECT PUTTING *Horton Smith & Dawson Taylor* 2.00
____SECRET OF SECRETS *U. S. Andersen* 2.00
____SECRETS OF HYPNOTISM *S. J. Van Pelt, M.D.* 2.00
____SEEING INTO THE FUTURE *Harvey Day* 2.00
____SELF-CONFIDENCE THROUGH SELF-ANALYSIS *E. Oakley* 1.00
____SELF-HYPNOSIS Its Theory, Technique & Application *Melvin Powers* 2.00
____SELF-HYPNOSIS A Conditioned-Response Technique *Laurance Sparks* 2.00
____7 DAYS TO FASTER READING *William S. Schaill* 2.00
____SEX AND HYPNOSIS *L. T. Woodward, M.D.* 2.00
____SEX WITHOUT GUILT *Albert Ellis, Ph.D.* 2.00
____SEXUALLY ADEQUATE FEMALE *Frank S. Caprio, M.D.* 1.75
____SEXUALLY ADEQUATE MALE *Frank S. Caprio, M.D.* 1.75
____STUDENT'S GUIDE TO EFFICIENT STUDY *D. E. Jones* 1.00
____SUCCESS-CYBERNETICS *U. S. Andersen* 2.00
____10 DAYS TO A GREAT NEW LIFE *William E. Edwards* 2.00
____THERAPY THROUGH HYPNOSIS *edited by Raphael H. Rhodes* 2.00
____THINK AND GROW RICH *Napoleon Hill* 2.00
____THOUGHT DIAL *Sydney Omarr* 2.00
____THREE MAGIC WORDS *U. S. Andersen* 2.00
____TREASURY OF COMFORT *edited by Rabbi Sidney Greenberg* 2.00
____TREASURY OF THE ART OF LIVING *edited by Rabbi S. Greenberg* 2.00
____VEGETARIAN COOKERY *Janet Walker* 2.00
____WITCHCRAFT–THE SIXTH SENSE *Justine Glass* 2.00
____YOU CAN ANALYZE HANDWRITING *Robert Holder* 2.00
____YOU CAN LEARN TO RELAX *Dr. Samuel Gutwirth* 1.00
____YOUR SUBCONSCIOUS POWER *Charles M. Simmons* 2.00
____YOUR THOUGHTS CAN CHANGE YOUR LIFE *Donald Curtis* 2.00

Notes

Notes